the BOYS in the
BASEMENT

CALIBER
COMICS

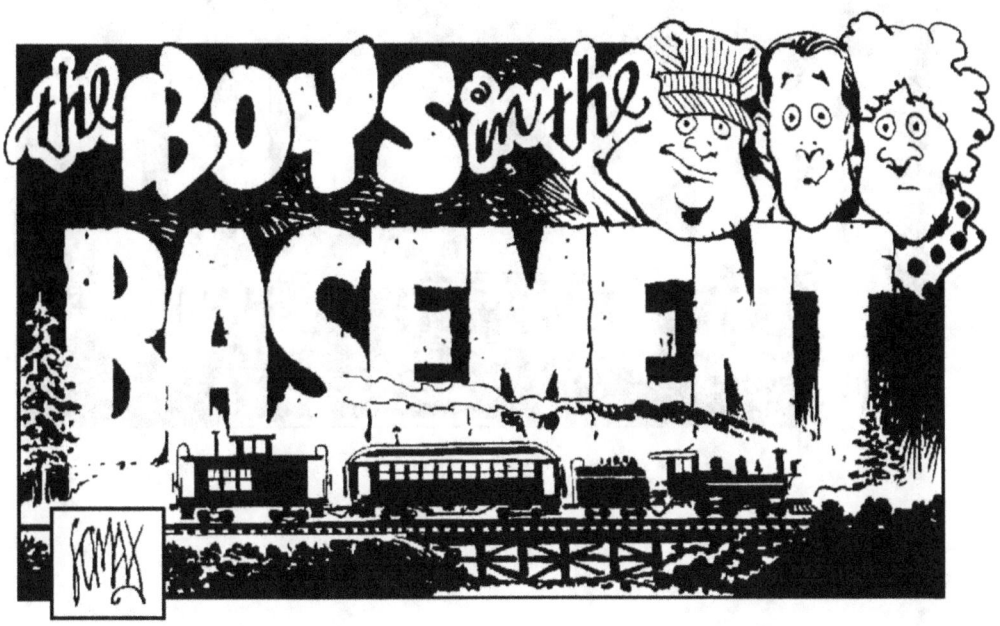

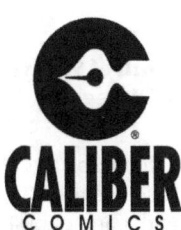

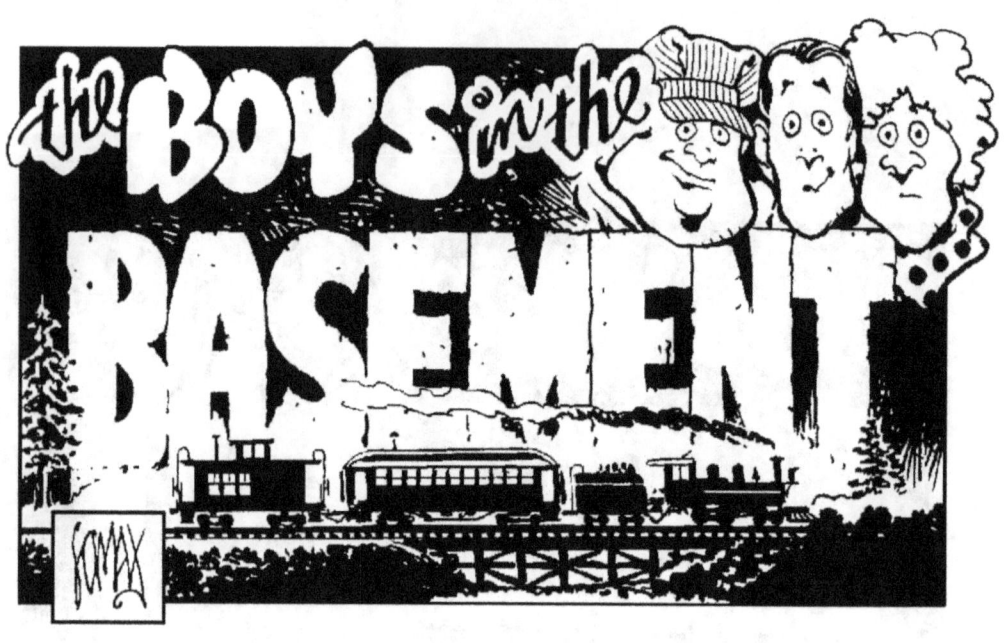

WRITTEN AND ILLUSTRATED
BY
DON LOMAX

ACKNOWLEDGEMENTS

THANKS TO:
Jim Reisdorff of South Platte Press
Jim Reese of Brueggenjohan/Reese Inc.

THE BOYS IN THE BASEMENT. COLLECTED EDITION. Published by Caliber Comics, a division of Caliber Entertainment LLC. Copyright 2022 Eagle One Media, Inc. All Rights Reserved. No part of this book may be copied or transmitted without the express written permission of the copyright holder and publisher. Limited use of art may be used for journalistic or review purposes. Any similarities to individuals either living or dead is purely coincidental and unintentional except where fair use laws apply. For more information please visit the Caliber Comics website: www.calibercomics.com

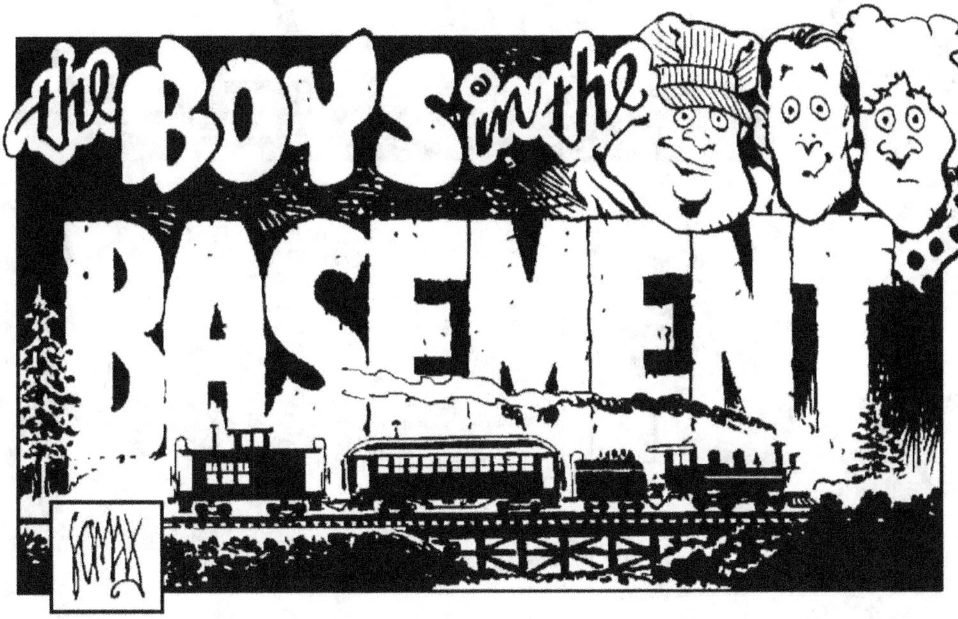
the BOYS in the
BASEMENT

COLLECTING "THE BOYS IN THE BASEMENT"
STRIP AS FEATURED IN THE PAGES OF
MODEL RAILROADING MAGAZINE

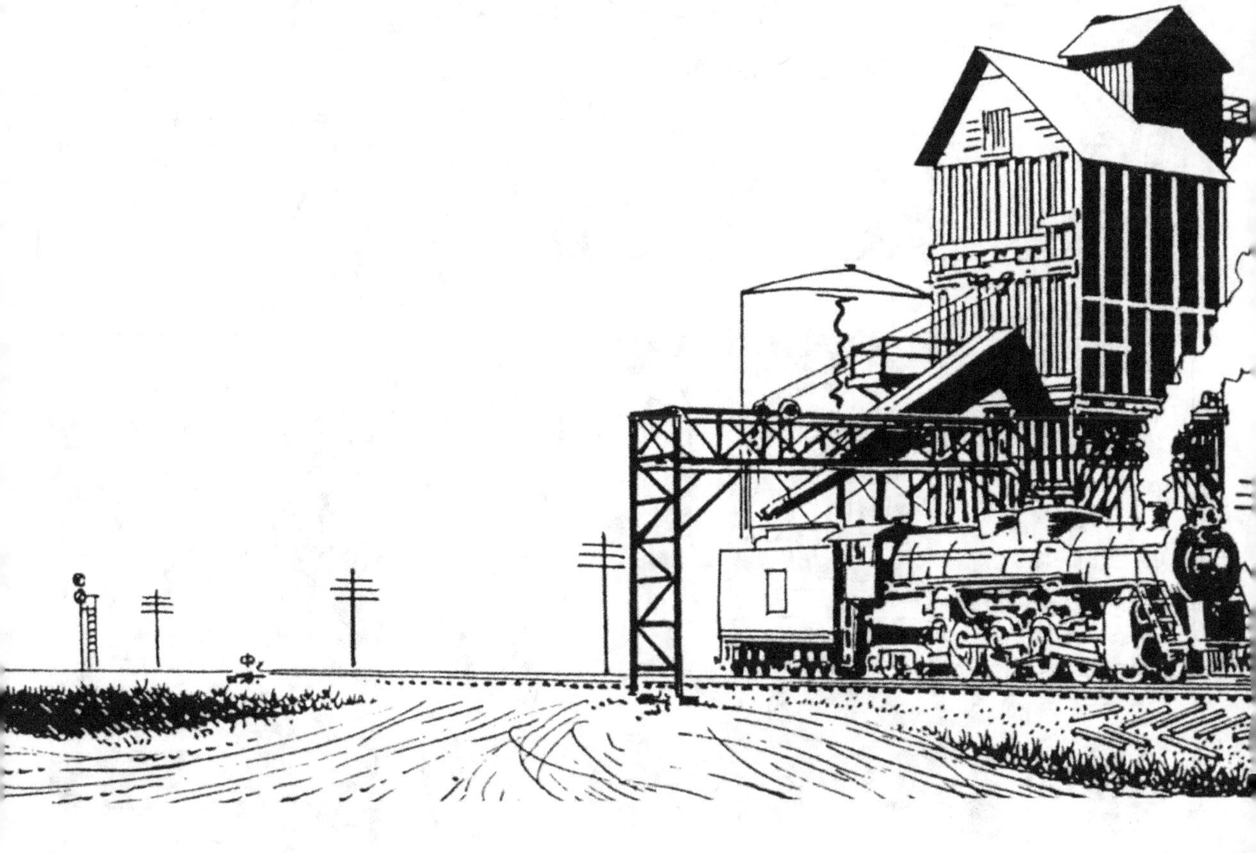

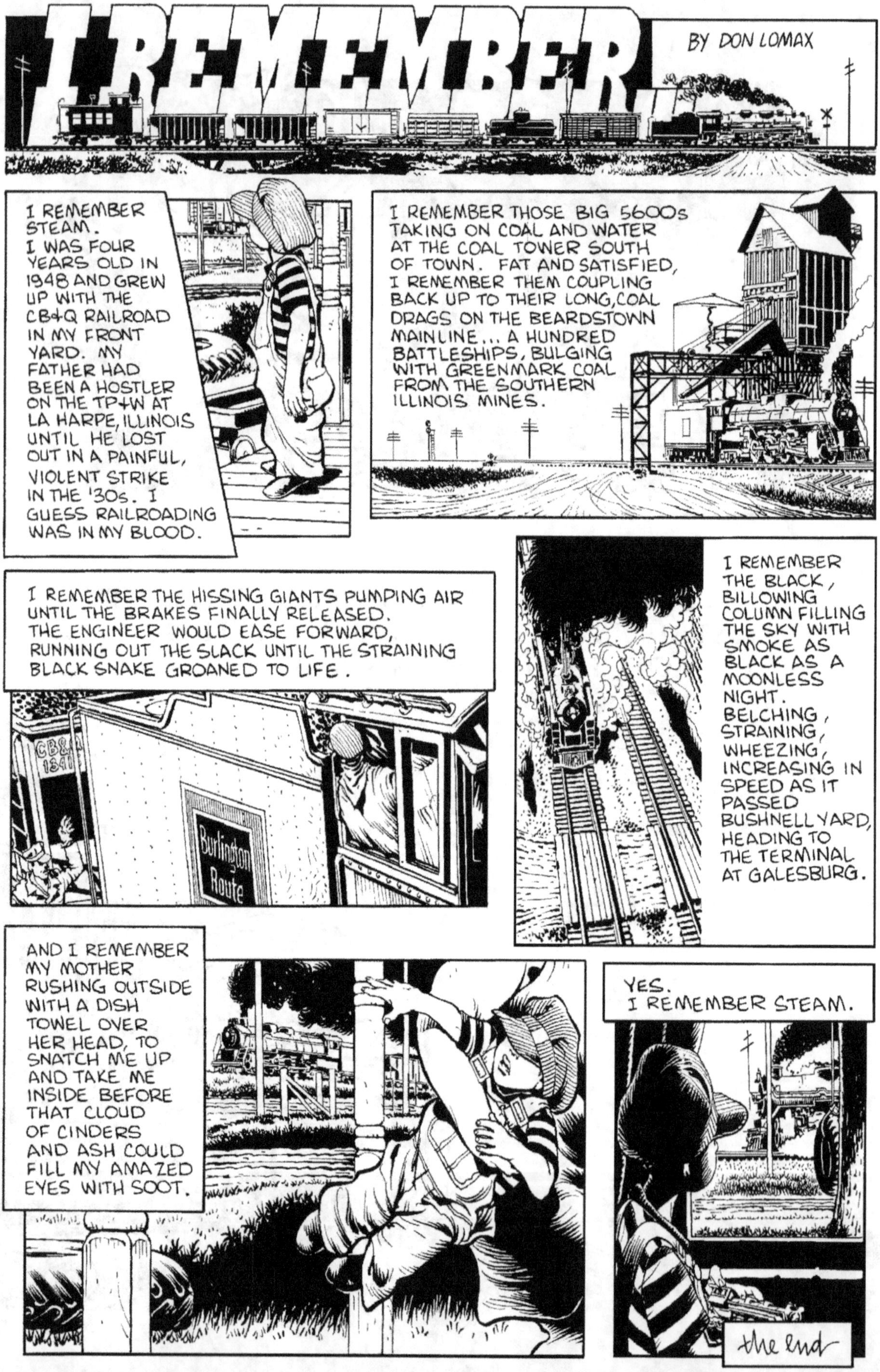
I REMEMBER...
BY DON LOMAX
I REMEMBER STEAM. I WAS FOUR YEARS OLD IN 1948 AND GREW UP WITH THE CB&Q RAILROAD IN MY FRONT YARD. MY FATHER HAD BEEN A HOSTLER ON THE TP&W AT LA HARPE, ILLINOIS UNTIL HE LOST OUT IN A PAINFUL, VIOLENT STRIKE IN THE '30s. I GUESS RAILROADING WAS IN MY BLOOD.
I REMEMBER THOSE BIG 5600s TAKING ON COAL AND WATER AT THE COAL TOWER SOUTH OF TOWN. FAT AND SATISFIED, I REMEMBER THEM COUPLING BACK UP TO THEIR LONG, COAL DRAGS ON THE BEARDSTOWN MAINLINE... A HUNDRED BATTLESHIPS, BULGING WITH GREENMARK COAL FROM THE SOUTHERN ILLINOIS MINES.
I REMEMBER THE HISSING GIANTS PUMPING AIR UNTIL THE BRAKES FINALLY RELEASED. THE ENGINEER WOULD EASE FORWARD, RUNNING OUT THE SLACK UNTIL THE STRAINING BLACK SNAKE GROANED TO LIFE.
CB&Q
Burlington Route
I REMEMBER THE BLACK, BILLOWING COLUMN FILLING THE SKY WITH SMOKE AS BLACK AS A MOONLESS NIGHT. BELCHING, STRAINING, WHEEZING, INCREASING IN SPEED AS IT PASSED BUSHNELL YARD, HEADING TO THE TERMINAL AT GALESBURG.
AND I REMEMBER MY MOTHER RUSHING OUTSIDE WITH A DISH TOWEL OVER HER HEAD, TO SNATCH ME UP AND TAKE ME INSIDE BEFORE THAT CLOUD OF CINDERS AND ASH COULD FILL MY AMAZED EYES WITH SOOT.
YES. I REMEMBER STEAM.
the end

The "Q" and the "Boys"

I was born in the latter days of World War II. Our country was making that last agonizing push into Nazi Germany in Europe, and taking the fight to the enemy from island to island in the Pacific in our relentless struggle to beat back the imperialistic Japanese.

In this country, the railroads were playing a primary roll in the transportation of goods and troops to supply the war effort. I was reared in my early impressionable years in Bushnell, Illinois, in the family house just across the street from the Chicago, Burlington & Quincy railroad yards.

As noted in the "I Remember..." comic strip on page four, the country's dependence on steam power and my memories of growing up in such a close proximity to the hissing, gigantic, friendly monsters of the steam era left an everlasting impression on the fertile mind of yours truly.

I was born to what would turn out to be a railroad family. My father was a hostler on the Toledo, Peoria & Western Railroad at La Harpe, Illinois, until he lost out in a heartbreaking strike in the '30s. It colored his outlook on life for the remainder of his years.

I have had two brother-in-laws who worked for railroads, one for the Chicago, Milwaukee, St. Paul & Pacific as a ticket agent and later a dispatcher, and the other for the CB&Q as an agent/operator and tower operator. I have a niece who is still a dispatcher for the Burlington Northern Santa Fe in Texas at present.

Through all of my school years I exhibited an interest in art and cartooning. However, when I graduated from high school I came to the shocking realization that drawing cute little pictures was a fun hobby, but it looked as though I was going to have to earn a living for the next 50 years. A realization that all young people must come to eventually...life isn't fair...I'm going to have to work for what I want out of life. Woe is me.

My brother-in-law on the "Q" offered to put in a good word for me with the trainmaster at Willis Yard, Galesburg, Illinois. I was hired and broke in at Seminary Street Tower. "Seminary" handled all trains coming into or leaving Galesburg in five directions; east to Chicago, north to Savanna, west to Ottumwa, south to Quincy and Beardstown, and east, again, to Peoria. Responsibilities for Seminary Tower included copying train orders and clearing northbound trains. The operation of the large interlocking plant through the depot area, in beautiful, downtown Galesburg, and the CTC boards for Waterman, Knox Street and Graham also fell under the umbrella of Seminary's responsibilities.

But, working on the extra board, I quickly found that one does not live by Seminary alone. After working my first day on February 29, 1964, Leap Year Day, I established my seniority in the job that would become a central part of my life for the next 20 years.

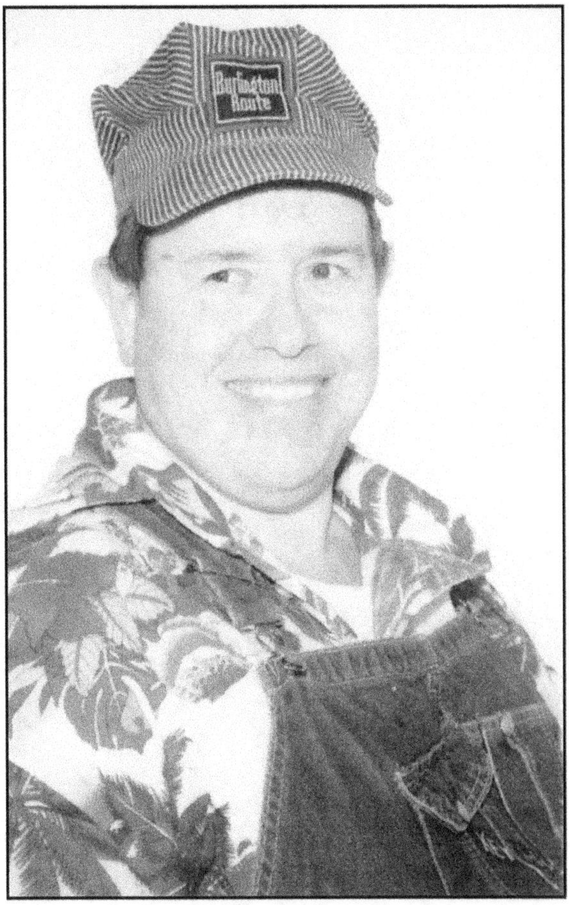
Burlington Route

Don Lomax. A remarkable resemblance to Merle, protangonist of "The Boys in the Basement."

For the next year and a half I posted and worked at the hump towers, learning to become a retarder operator at Willis, the east and west classification yard in Galesburg.

My railroad career was rudely interrupted in the fall of 1965 with a letter from the draft board. It read as follows;

"Greetings, your friends and neighbors have selected you to serve a short term in the armed forces of your country. Serve proudly."

My propensity and fondness for my art hobby was pretty much put on hold for the next two years. I went into the Army, spent a tour in Vietnam and returned home to my job on the "Q."

The railroad in the Sixties was suffering from an identity crisis. The transition to diesel power had been completed. On the rare occasion that one of the Burlington's remaining steam excursion engines would make a run, it was, even then, an oddity and the focus of awe-inspired stares. When I

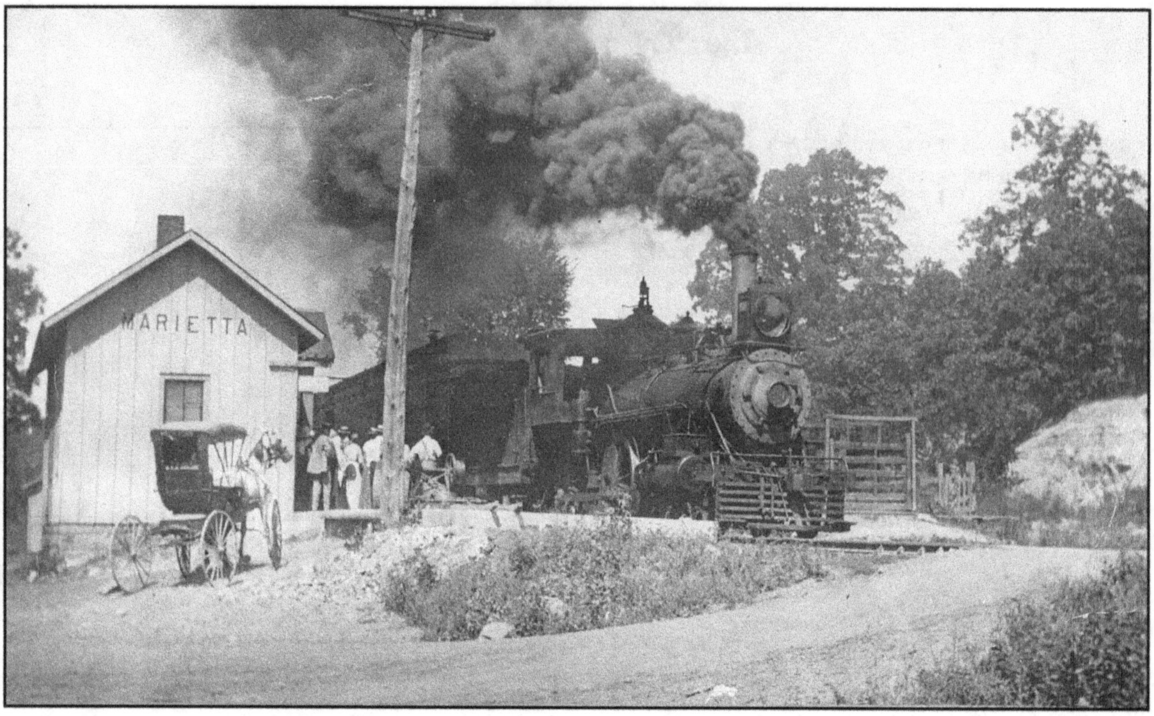
MARIETTA

My father's railroad: the Toledo, Peoria & Western at Marietta, Illinois. A vintage 4-4-0 steam locomotive pulls up to the depot with a passenger train during the days of straw hats and horse-drawn buggies.

spent time with the "old-timers," the stories of the age of steam stirred a yearning in me that most of my brethren of the High Iron felt deep down in our souls for all their days. I then understood my father's lifetime longing to belong to something as significant as a career in railroading.

Telephones had replaced the telegraph. The changing face of the railroad was long and agonizing, but change came as the country advanced toward the computer age like a drunk crawling home over broken bottles.

In those days I married and, with my first wife, had five children, one died. I was working third trick at "C" Tower, the east hump at Willis, and my need to draw cartoons had again came to the forefront. Anyone with small children knows that some of our most peaceful times are not in the house, and I would often look forward to my quiet time at work. I always carried my briefcase with my drawing supplies with me and scratched out cartoon after cartoon continually during lulls in my railroad duties. Although not exactly approved of by railroad policy, I always rationalized that it was better that I occupy myself thus rather than sleeping on the job as most of my co-workers did. There was one co-worker of mine who bragged that he had worked third trick for 26 years and never missed a night's sleep.

I would like to take this opportunity to thank the railroad for the years of providing me with a quiet studio atmosphere to develop what artistic skills I have acquired over the years. There was no rent involved and they gave me a good excuse to retreat with regularity to indulge in my love for cartooning. I must admit there were times when I felt a little guilty on the drive to work, leaving my wife to wrestle with the kids while I escaped to the entertaining world of cartoons and comics. "Well, better her than me," as we used to say in the 'Nam.

In 1975 a job opened in my home town of Bushnell. The previous agent/operator job at the Bushnell depot was being expanded to an around-the-clock operation with the addition of a second and third trick operator, with a swing job to include the extra day at Seminary Tower. That swing job was right up my alley. I bid on it and won.

The Burlington Northern (by then the"Q" was history) had contracted to deliver, via the TP&W at Bushnell, unit coal trains to Illinois Power at their electrical generating plant in Havana, Illinois. I expanded my art studio to include the Bushnell depot, a quiet, well-lit place to do my cartoons. Thanks again, BN Railroad.

It was around that time that I sold my first, one page, black and white comic strip to a national publication... "Puttin' With The Rat" for *Easyriders* magazine. It became a semi-regular addition to the motorcycle magazine and whetted my appetite for the sweet checks and reader adulation of the professional magazine cartoonist.

Over the next few years my cartoons and comics appeared in numerous national magazines. My double life seemed to suit me fine, though a couple of incidents stand out. Both involved snow—lots of it.

Incident No. 1 occurred in the pre-Amtrak era. We had been dealing with blizzard conditions for the past week. Work found me at Seminary Tower, where the movement of trains that entire week had been a nightmare. The passenger trains, of course, had priority and even so were running late, sometimes by several hours.

Number 3, due in Galesburg during second shift, was just out of Chicago when I relieved my brother-in-law, Louie Paxton, the regular second trick operator. I was lucky to have made it. The wind was blowing at blizzard conditions, filling the power switches faster than the section hands could sweep them clean.

The brass were having a fit. Number 3 was having all kinds of trouble with heat and air problems. The delays were stacking up. At Aurora they tried to beat the ice out of the lines. At Sandwich another delay. Kewanee, another nearly two hours. All of the time we were battling the switch problems. Every time I reversed a switch I had no guarantee I would get a confirmation light that the switches were up tight and safe for movement.

On the big interlocking plant it would take, sometimes, a dozen tries to get the lever to click that sweet "click" which allowed the handle to be pulled out completely, indicating a successful switch alignment.

The terminal superintendent, Mr. L.H. Dyer, himself, was down on the depot platform barking orders and running the show.

"Seminary Tower!" His unmistakable, gruff voice crackled on the intercom.

"Seminary," says I in response.

"We're losing ground down here." He admitted defeat. If you knew Mr. L. H. Dyer you would have known how unusual that was, and in addition, he did not feel the need to blame everyone under him through his frustration. I think it was just too cold even for him to criticize. Believe me, that's cold.

"Get a hold of the section foreman...have him and his people start at the east end of the plant, line up for Number 3, and have him spike the switches all the way through town. If we get nothing else done tonight, maybe we can get 3 through town."

I acknowledged with a click of the intercom peddle, as was

Following the view on the opposite page, No. 6 is stopped at the Galesburg depot to load passengers and change crews before continuing on to Chicago. The fluted tail end observation car included a viewing dome for passenger's enjoyment.

the custom, and the mission was accomplished as though we were obeying the word of God.

Number 3 finally limped into town too late to even matter. It was the one thing we needed to accomplish. Finally, with a new crew, Number 3 rolled out of town heading west in a swirl of snow and to the relief of all involved.

As quiet again descended, I breathed a sigh. The florescent light flickered, the radio murmured in the background the incoherent babble of one yard engine to another out in the yard, and I was beginning to think about making another pot of coffee to go with the Hostess cherry pie I had packed in my lunch. Life was good.

Seminary Tower was a two-story structure. The bottom floor was the maintainer's office and housed the relays and mechanical devices that gave the signals and switches the impulses to make the whole plant work. The second floor held the interlocking plant and was the office of the tower operator on duty. Running up the back, or east side of the tower, was an open stairway common to when the tower was built, which led to the second floor of the building. It was a noisy, steel contraption and one could usually hear the approach of any visitor. But, the wind was howling and the snow muffled any footsteps.

The first time I was aware of the invasion was when the door burst open and a large, black figure rushed inside and closed the door behind him before I could even regret the fact that I had not locked it earlier in my shift. We often locked the door on third trick as a precaution against just such an intrusion. But with sectionmen in the area sweeping switches, I often left the door unlocked as a courtesy so they might come in and warm up on nights such as those.

Suddenly the biggest, maddest, most unpleasant individual it had been my misfortune to confront since Vietnam was standing, fuming beside the desk where I was sitting.

Again the intercom crackled to life, but this time it was Rudy, the section foreman.

"Seminary, you're gonna have a visitor. Some guy was suppose to get on Number 3, but he didn't get here in time. Better lock your door! He's madder'n a wet hen!"

I swallowed hard and keyed the mike. "Thanks, Rudy. He's standing right here beside the desk."

There was a pause. "Sorry...can I have your car?"

Apparently Rudy thought I was a dead man.

The next 15 minutes were filled with a tirade of expletives and jailhouse jargon that would confuse all but the most hardcore habitual, repeat offender. The gist of it seemed to be that he had come into town on the Santa Fe passenger train earlier in the evening for a connection to take Number 3 to Burlington, Iowa, where his baby-momma lived.

He had just gotten out of Joliet State Prison, doing a dime for armed robbery and assault with a deadly weapon. He said that a shive was his weapon of choice and proceeded to show me an ugly-looking blade with USMC stamped on it up next to the hilt. It was a Kabar, the knife of choice for the Marine Corps—though I doubted he got it through service to his country.

He continued. I am paraphrasing now since I could never repeat the dialogue of the foul-mouthed exchange that spewed out of his gold-toothed mouth in a never-ending river of filth. But the condensed version is as follows: Apparently, he had gotten off the Santa Fe hotshot at the Santa Fe depot a mile across town and asked the ticket agent how Number 3 was running. He was told our train was three to four hours late. So on his way to the BN depot he hit every bar that was open, and trust me, that is several.

Even though he showed up at the BN depot nearly five hours later, he still considered it the BN's fault that he missed his connection, and since I was the BN representative handy in front of him, my fault.

There were several less than veiled threats that someone was going to pay with their blood before the night was over. And since I did not think I could spare any blood on a cold night like that, I had to think of a way out of that particular situation.

"It looks to me like that ticket agent over at the Santa Fe steered you wrong, man."

"Uh...?"

"Sure...if he'd given you better information you wouldn't have missed your connection and you'd be on your way to your lady right now. That guy really gave you the shaft." I spun for all I was worth. "If anybody deserves to bleed it is that guy."

He looked confused, in an alcoholic haze sort of way. "Yeah, the (expletive)."

As he turned and lumbered back out into the cold to return to the Santa Fe depot to extract his pound of revenge I locked the door behind him. I knew that the Santa Fe ticket agent was long gone home and the depot locked up tight by then.

"Go get him, man..." says I, with a sigh of relief.

I immediately called the BN special agent and Galesburg city police and told them the story. I saw Rudy a couple of days later. He did not really say so, but I think he had a whole new respect for my ability to weasel out of a ticklish situation.

He never did get my car.

Incident No. 2 occurred during a repeat performance by Mother Nature known as the Blizzard of '79.

This January storm had closed all of the roads and isolated each community in West Central Illinois unto itself. I was working as third shift operator at the Bushnell depot. Nothing was running except the Amtrak passenger trains,

Max Lindstrom was the day operator at Seminary Street Tower at Galesburg for many years. Here, wearing an old agent's hat for fun, Max uses the tower's telegraph system. Although there was no requirement by the late 1960s that operators use the telegraph, it gave oldtimers who knew telegraphy another method of talk when the phones were busy.

and they with great difficulty. Number 347 (the "Illinois Zephyr") was due to pass through Bushnell at 9:25 pm the night before, but the usual air and heat problems kept pushing the time back into the wee hours of the morning.

Number 347 did not stop at Bushnell. The closest stop was Macomb, but with the roads closed it may as well have been the moon.

The trainmaster at Willis Yard called me during my shift at Bushnell with a strange story that had been reported to him by the conductor of Number 3, the 347's parent train. It seemed, according to the conductor, an unnamed woman out of Chicago had to get off the train at Bushnell. It was a confused, muddled story. Either she was an emergency blood donor for some poor desperate soul and doctors and patient were waiting for her in Bushnell, or her blood donor was in Bushnell and she was in desperate need, or she needed some life saving treatment that only Bushnell could provide.

Bushnell?

As far as I was concerned, this story did not pass the smell test. But the BN's great minds working that night were all convinced it was a legitimate emergency. Who am I to argue with the chief dispatchers of two divisions and the duty trainmaster at Galesburg?

This night 347 would make an emergency stop in Bushnell.

Since the Bushnell depot was no longer a passenger station and not accessible to the public as it were, the depot platform had not been cleared of three feet of snow drifts and ice from the blizzard. This might represent a hazard for a sick or medically-delicate passenger to dismount the train at the station.

I made an innocent suggestion to Frank, the second trick Hannibal dispatcher. Perhaps dismounting at the depot might not be the best idea for the lady. I suggested the train spot the car with her at the Davis Street crossing 100 yards or so north of the depot. It had been cleared by snow plows earlier. Likewise, I suggested, perhaps I should ask the local police to meet the train and help her off in case they might be needed on the slippery grade crossing. An innocuous request that would soon snowball (pun intended) out of control.

The chief dispatcher chimed in, saying he would take care of it. Perhaps it was the fact that everyone working that night had a lot of spare time on their hands, due to the fact that not much in the form of trains were moving throughout the division.

In Galesburg, Number 3 had finally arrived on track 3 at the depot among swirling snow and crews were changed. The story of the emergency lady grew, as it was, passed by word of mouth to 347's conductor. The switch crew coupled onto what was soon to become 347's train off the rear end of Number 3 and sat it to 5 track and the waiting diesel unit that was to make up the Hannibal Division train.

In Bushnell, a city police officer showed up at the depot and through the ticket window I explained the situation as it was explained to me.

In Galesburg, 347 was having trouble getting its air and heat again was a problem.

In Bushnell, two more local cops showed up and again I explained.

The snow swirled, the temperature dropped, and through the frosted depot window flashing emergency lights of every color of the rainbow descended on the depot. All I wanted was someone to help the lady off the train. It was rapidly turning into a circus.

Another city cop, four firemen, two paramedics, and an Illinois State Trooper filed into my waiting room. I tried to explain to each new arrival the situation and brewed coffee. Then I brewed more coffee. And more. I was starting to feel like a waitress at a truckstop diner as the morning stretched on.

I suggested some of them might go home. They would have none of it. Faithful public servants all, they would all see it through to the bitter end. I harmonized to the dispatcher, he pretended he was busy.

The view from Seminary. Train No. 35's sleek CB&Q passenger unit waits to back onto its train on track 5 at the Galesburg depot while a northbound freight departs on the outbound freight track at right. This shot was taken from the north window of Seminary Street Tower.

Finally, the third trick operator at the Galesburg depot OSed the train. 347 was out of Galesburg and on its miserable way. Preparations were made. All of the rescue personnel on hand checked their equipment, put on their gear, turned in their coffee cups, and emptied out of the depot to position themselves to wait.

347 drifted into town in the usual swirl of snow and squeaked to a halt.

A small, dark figure stepped down from the train unassisted, crossed quickly to a waiting car, and the car drove off. It took, maybe, half a minute.

We'd been hornswaggled.

The bevy of public servants who's time could have been better spent somewhere else that frigid, January morning were, to say the least, perturbed.

The chief dispatchers and Galesburg trainmaster suddenly got amnesia about their involvment in the fiasco. Somehow it became all my fault. The railroad was dodging responsibility. The local city counsel threatened law suits and I avoided irate phone calls for a month. There was talk about prosecution of the lady hoaxer. I do not know whether it was followed up on or not.

The Blizzard of '79 was a hoot.

In 1982 the Bushnell station went back to just the first shift agent/operator and I bumped in to the swing job at "B" Tower, East Hump, Willis Yard. I was a "retarded" operator again.

In 1984 the BN was offering buy-outs to get rid of deadwood; jobs which were protected under the CB&Q/Northern Pacific merger years earlier. I felt that this was an excellent opportunity to change my life and pursue my first love, cartooning. That was 20 years ago, and though we had some lean times, I never regretted the decision...though I sometimes got a little nostalgic around the 13th and 28th of the month.

I continued with my magazine work doing adult cartoons, comic strips for *CARtoons*, *Easyriders*, and several comic book publishers, including Pacific, First, Apple, and Marvel. I created *Vietnam Journal*, a comic for Apple Comics which ran several years, and I got the opportunity to write Marvel's popular *The 'Nam* comic for a few years.

During the summer of 1998, I happened to be in our local hobby shop and a copy of *Model Railroading* magazine caught my eye. I bought a copy and took it home. It was slick and cool, but I determined it was missing a key component. A comic strip by yours truly.

I sat down at my drawing board and created "The Boys in

the Basement," a comic strip about three model railroading devotees, Merle, Earl, and Lenny. I sent it in to Randy Lee, the editor, on speculation and he was kind enough to run the strip in the magazine where it has appeared ever since.

The following is a collection of those strips. I hope you enjoy them.

Don Lomax

P.S. - People often ask me if I am a model railroader. I have a great interest but no time. I love to draw too much and a layout is a time-consuming labor of love if it is done right. Maybe some day... But in the meantime, I must comfort myself in the knowledge that I spent 20 years with access to quite an impressive layout, scale 1:1. I still have dreams about missed switches and horiffic derailments from those exciting railroad days.

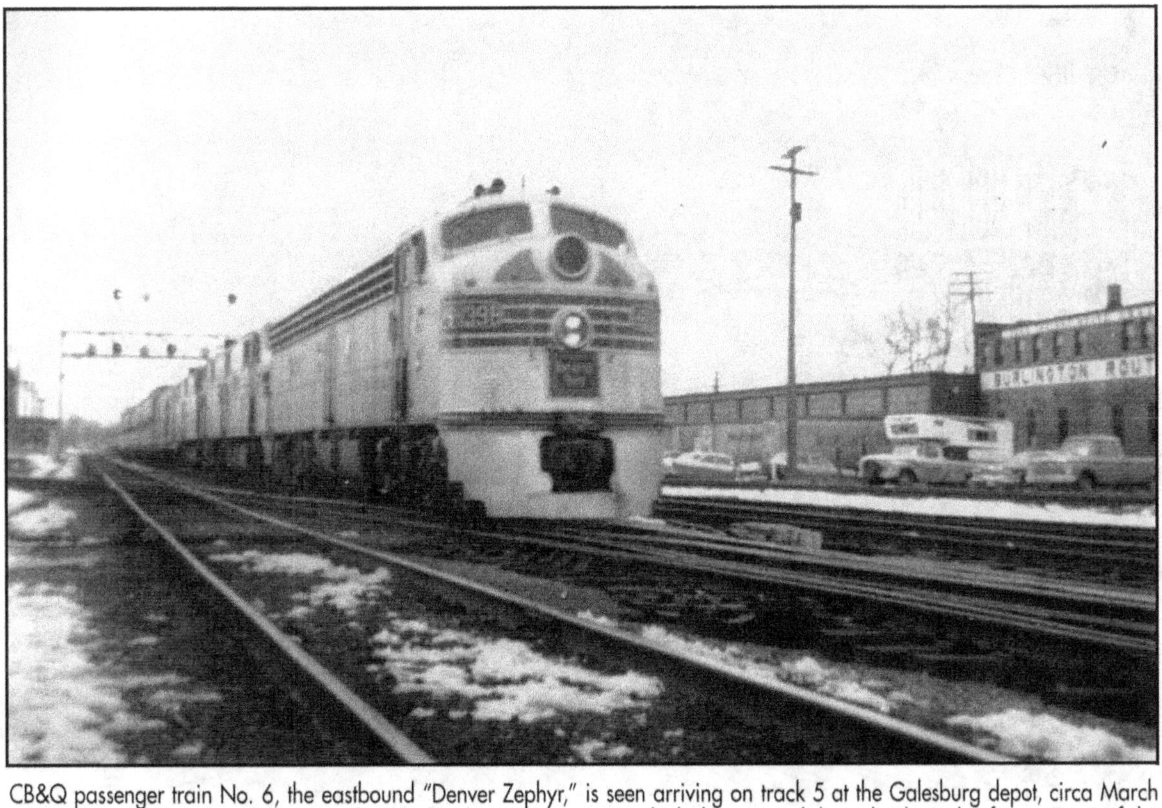
BURLINGTON ROUTE
CB&Q passenger train No. 6, the eastbound "Denver Zephyr," is seen arriving on track 5 at the Galesburg depot, circa March 1965. This was just one of a series of streamlined passenger trains which then passed through "the Hub of Lines East" of the Burlington Route.

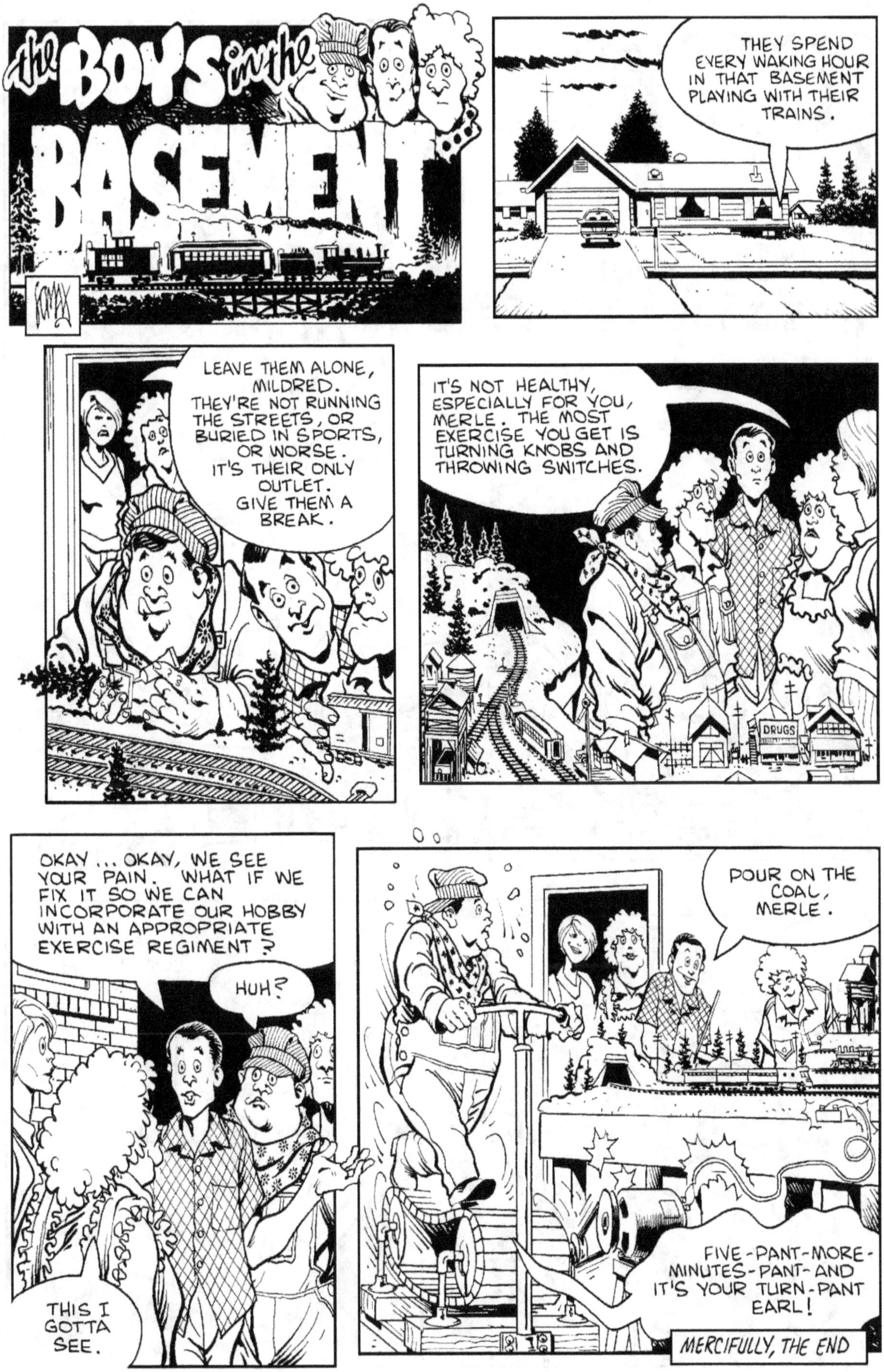
the BOYS in the BASEMENT
THEY SPEND EVERY WAKING HOUR IN THAT BASEMENT PLAYING WITH THEIR TRAINS.
LEAVE THEM ALONE, MILDRED. THEY'RE NOT RUNNING THE STREETS, OR BURIED IN SPORTS, OR WORSE. IT'S THEIR ONLY OUTLET. GIVE THEM A BREAK.
IT'S NOT HEALTHY, ESPECIALLY FOR YOU, MERLE. THE MOST EXERCISE YOU GET IS TURNING KNOBS AND THROWING SWITCHES.
DRUGS
OKAY ... OKAY, WE SEE YOUR PAIN. WHAT IF WE FIX IT SO WE CAN INCORPORATE OUR HOBBY WITH AN APPROPRIATE EXERCISE REGIMENT?
HUH?
THIS I GOTTA SEE.
POUR ON THE COAL, MERLE.
FIVE-PANT-MORE-MINUTES-PANT-AND IT'S YOUR TURN-PANT EARL!
MERCIFULLY, THE END

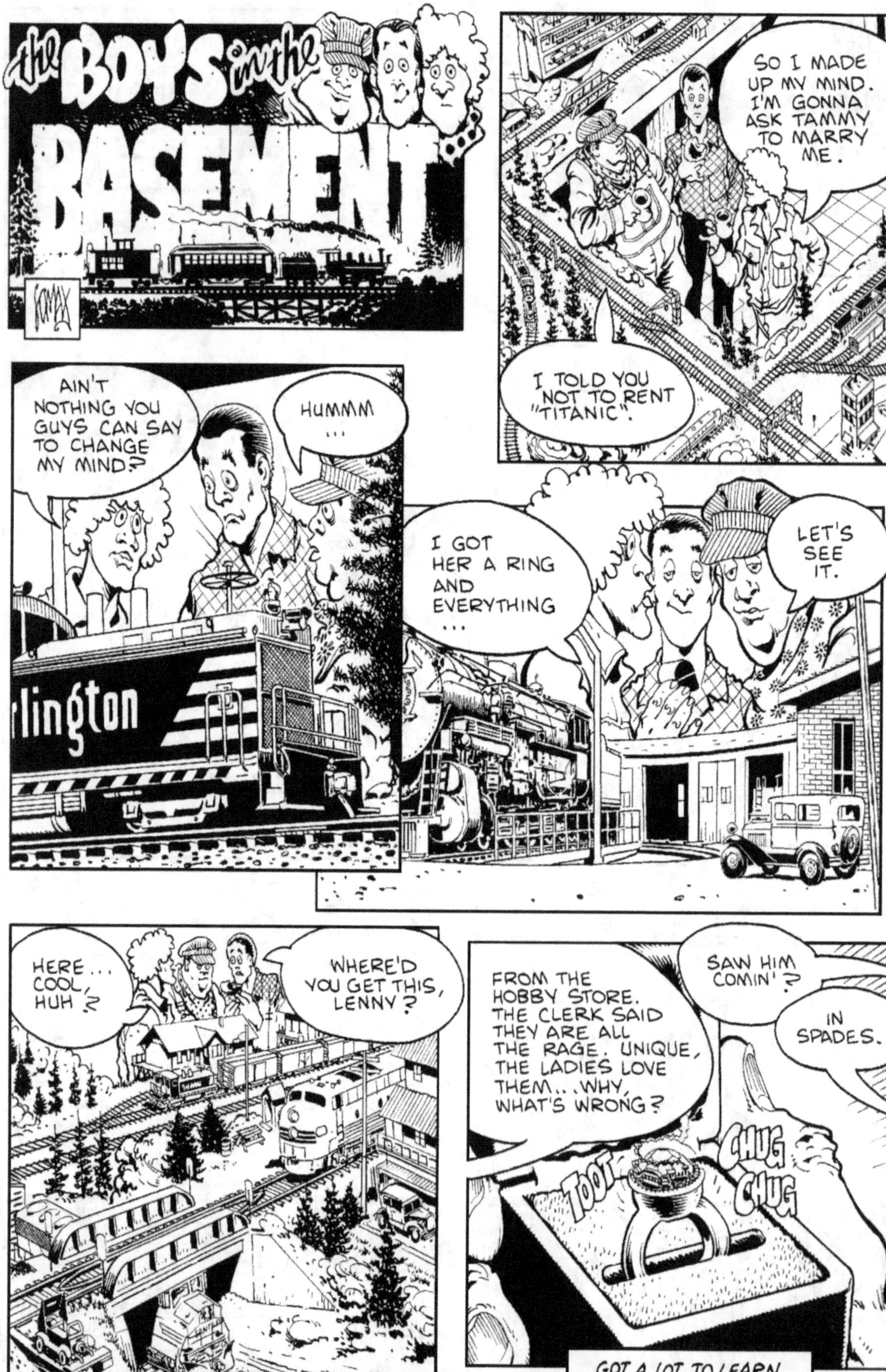
the BOYS in the BASEMENT
SO I MADE UP MY MIND. I'M GONNA ASK TAMMY TO MARRY ME.
I TOLD YOU NOT TO RENT "TITANIC".
AIN'T NOTHING YOU GUYS CAN SAY TO CHANGE MY MIND?
HUMMM ...
rlington
I GOT HER A RING AND EVERYTHING ...
LET'S SEE IT.
HERE... COOL, HUH?
WHERE'D YOU GET THIS, LENNY?
FROM THE HOBBY STORE. THE CLERK SAID THEY ARE ALL THE RAGE. UNIQUE, THE LADIES LOVE THEM... WHY, WHAT'S WRONG?
SAW HIM COMIN'?
IN SPADES.
TOOT
CHUG CHUG
GOT A LOT TO LEARN.

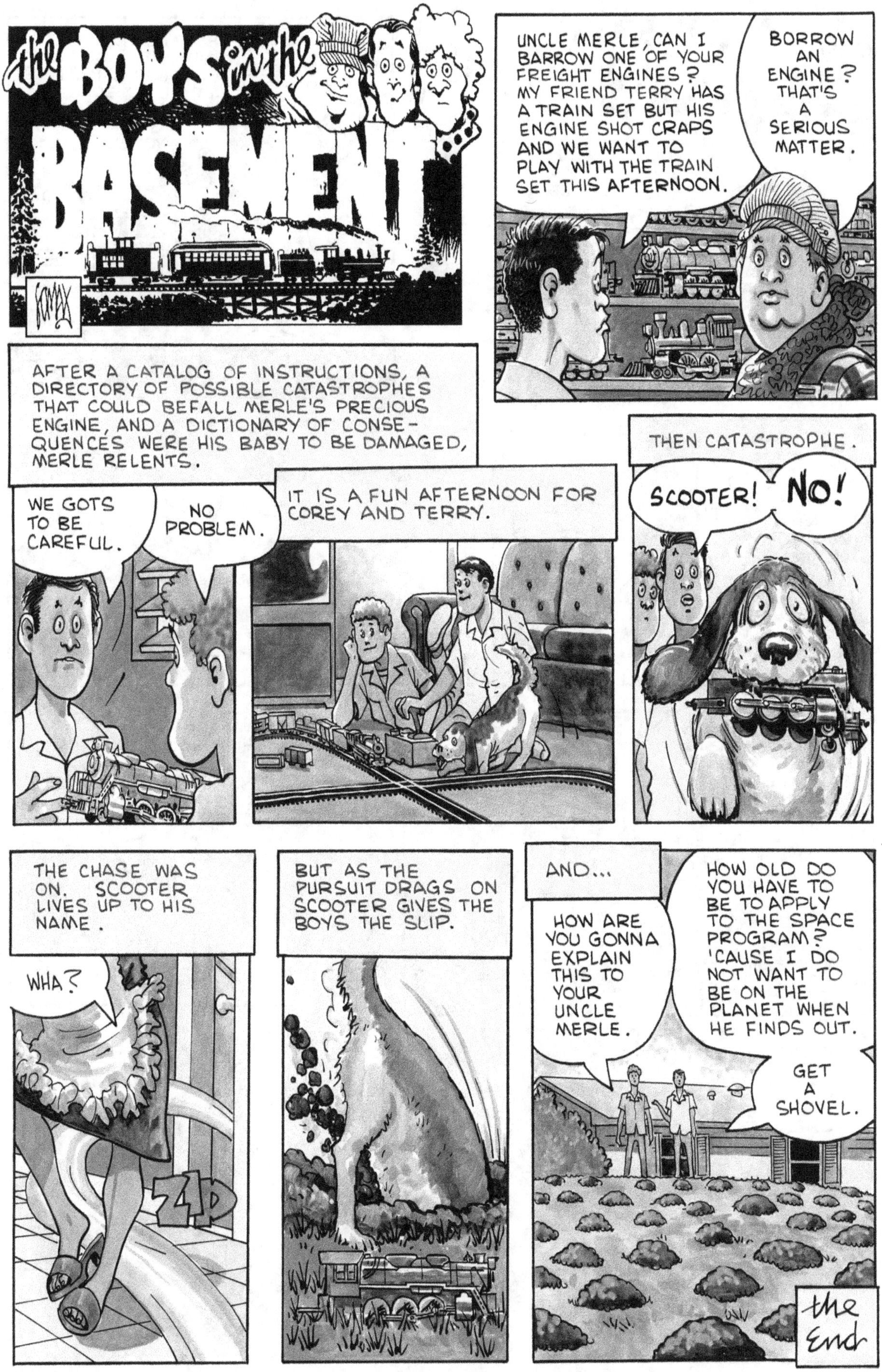
the BOYS in the BASEMENT
UNCLE MERLE, CAN I BARROW ONE OF YOUR FREIGHT ENGINES ? MY FRIEND TERRY HAS A TRAIN SET BUT HIS ENGINE SHOT CRAPS AND WE WANT TO PLAY WITH THE TRAIN SET THIS AFTERNOON.
BORROW AN ENGINE ? THAT'S A SERIOUS MATTER.
AFTER A CATALOG OF INSTRUCTIONS, A DIRECTORY OF POSSIBLE CATASTROPHES THAT COULD BEFALL MERLE'S PRECIOUS ENGINE, AND A DICTIONARY OF CONSE-QUENCES WERE HIS BABY TO BE DAMAGED, MERLE RELENTS.
WE GOTS TO BE CAREFUL.
NO PROBLEM.
IT IS A FUN AFTERNOON FOR COREY AND TERRY.
THEN CATASTROPHE.
SCOOTER!
NO!
THE CHASE WAS ON. SCOOTER LIVES UP TO HIS NAME.
WHA?
ZIP
BUT AS THE PURSUIT DRAGS ON SCOOTER GIVES THE BOYS THE SLIP.
AND...
HOW ARE YOU GONNA EXPLAIN THIS TO YOUR UNCLE MERLE.
HOW OLD DO YOU HAVE TO BE TO APPLY TO THE SPACE PROGRAM? 'CAUSE I DO NOT WANT TO BE ON THE PLANET WHEN HE FINDS OUT.
GET A SHOVEL.
the End

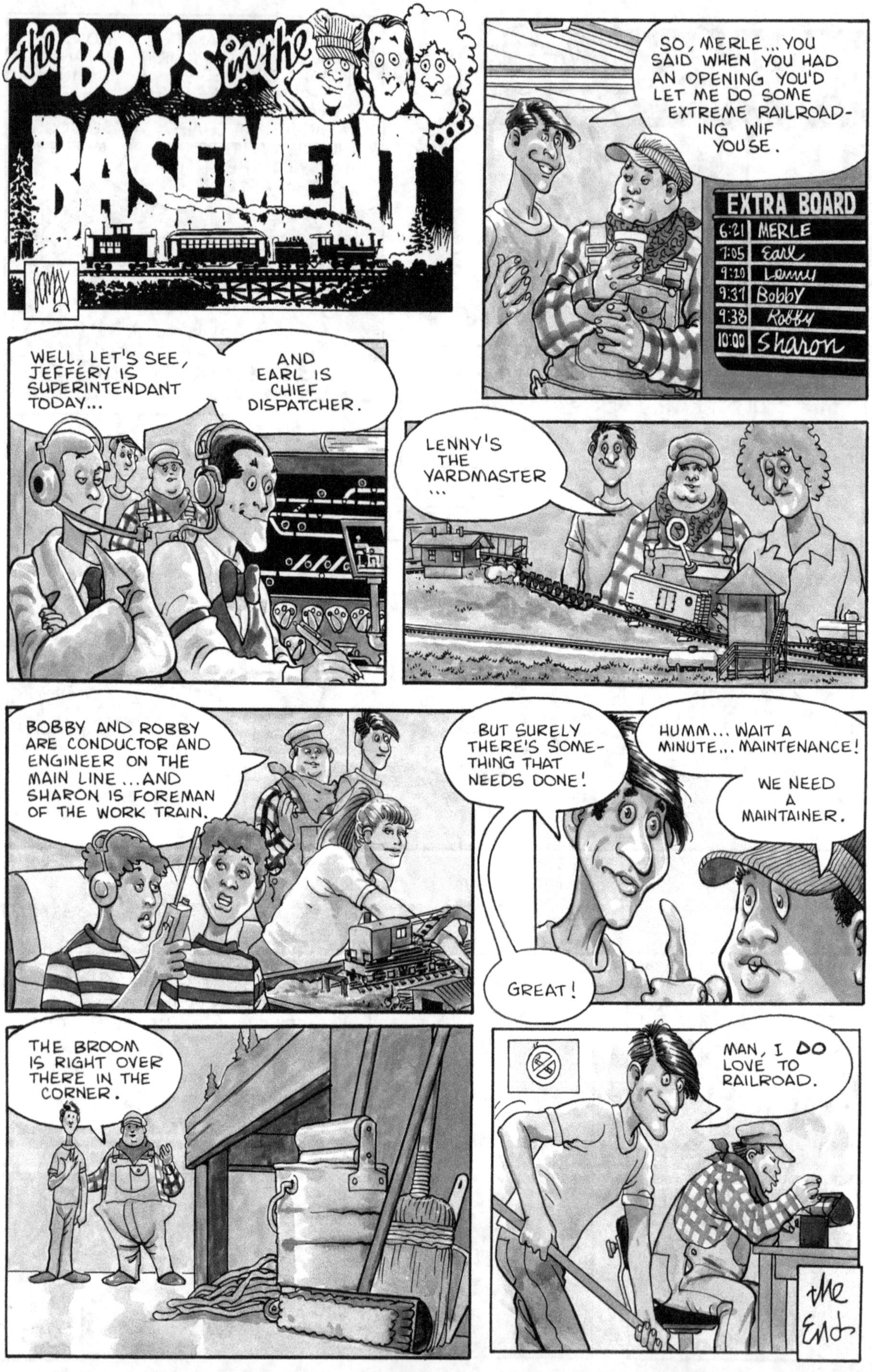
the BOYS in the BASEMENT
SO, MERLE... YOU SAID WHEN YOU HAD AN OPENING YOU'D LET ME DO SOME EXTREME RAILROADING WIF YOUSE.
EXTRA BOARD
6:21 MERLE
7:05 Earl
9:20 Lenny
9:37 Bobby
9:38 Robby
10:00 Sharon
WELL, LET'S SEE, JEFFERY IS SUPERINTENDANT TODAY...
AND EARL IS CHIEF DISPATCHER.
LENNY'S THE YARDMASTER ...
BOBBY AND ROBBY ARE CONDUCTOR AND ENGINEER ON THE MAIN LINE ... AND SHARON IS FOREMAN OF THE WORK TRAIN.
BUT SURELY THERE'S SOMETHING THAT NEEDS DONE!
HUMM... WAIT A MINUTE... MAINTENANCE!
WE NEED A MAINTAINER.
GREAT!
THE BROOM IS RIGHT OVER THERE IN THE CORNER.
MAN, I DO LOVE TO RAILROAD.
the End

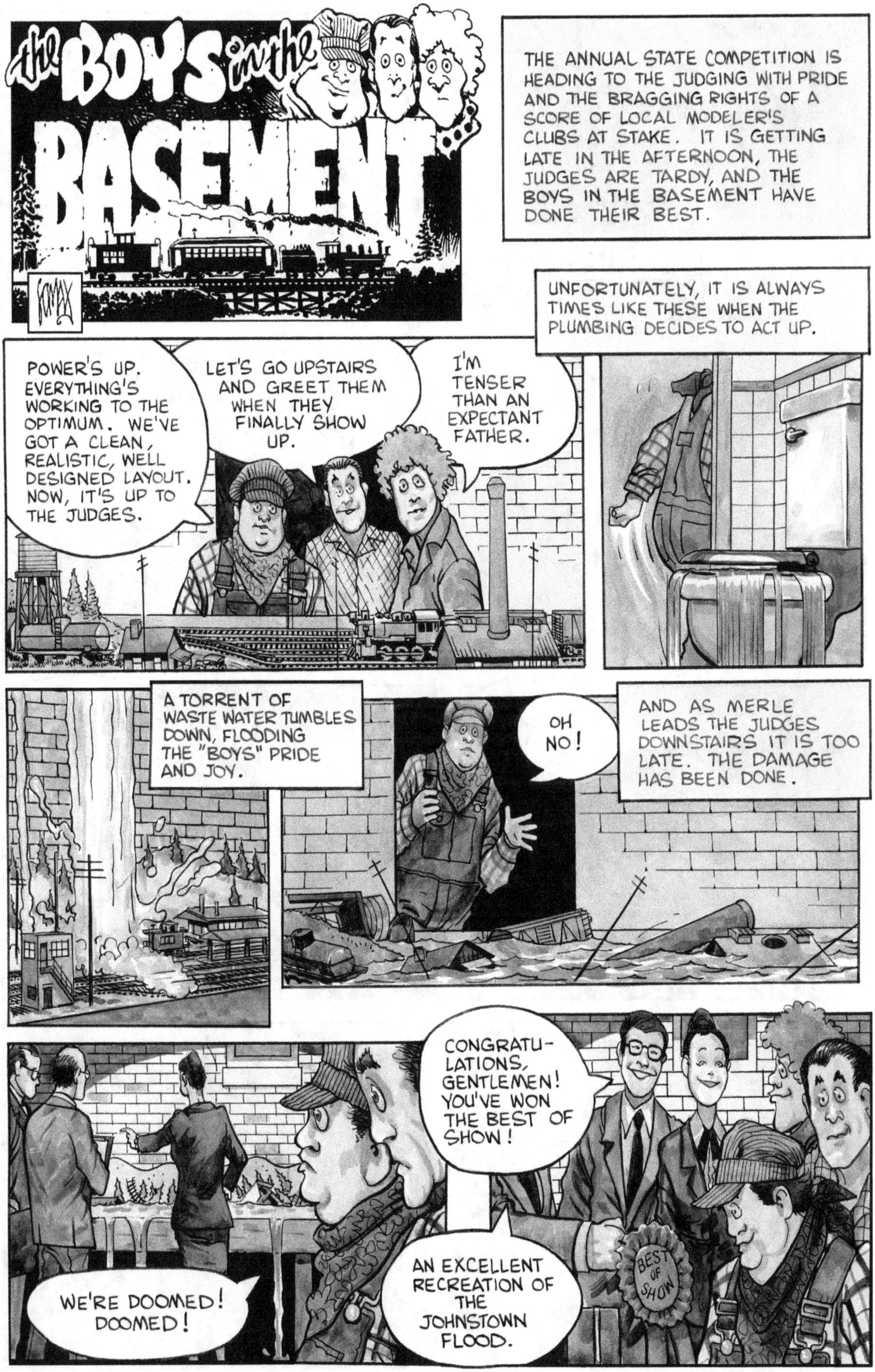
the BOYS in the BASEMENT
THE ANNUAL STATE COMPETITION IS HEADING TO THE JUDGING WITH PRIDE AND THE BRAGGING RIGHTS OF A SCORE OF LOCAL MODELER'S CLUBS AT STAKE. IT IS GETTING LATE IN THE AFTERNOON, THE JUDGES ARE TARDY, AND THE BOYS IN THE BASEMENT HAVE DONE THEIR BEST.
POWER'S UP. EVERYTHING'S WORKING TO THE OPTIMUM. WE'VE GOT A CLEAN, REALISTIC, WELL DESIGNED LAYOUT. NOW, IT'S UP TO THE JUDGES.
LET'S GO UPSTAIRS AND GREET THEM WHEN THEY FINALLY SHOW UP.
I'M TENSER THAN AN EXPECTANT FATHER.
UNFORTUNATELY, IT IS ALWAYS TIMES LIKE THESE WHEN THE PLUMBING DECIDES TO ACT UP.
A TORRENT OF WASTE WATER TUMBLES DOWN, FLOODING THE "BOYS" PRIDE AND JOY.
OH NO!
AND AS MERLE LEADS THE JUDGES DOWNSTAIRS IT IS TOO LATE. THE DAMAGE HAS BEEN DONE.
WE'RE DOOMED! DOOMED!
CONGRATULATIONS, GENTLEMEN! YOU'VE WON THE BEST OF SHOW!
AN EXCELLENT RECREATION OF THE JOHNSTOWN FLOOD.
BEST OF SHOW

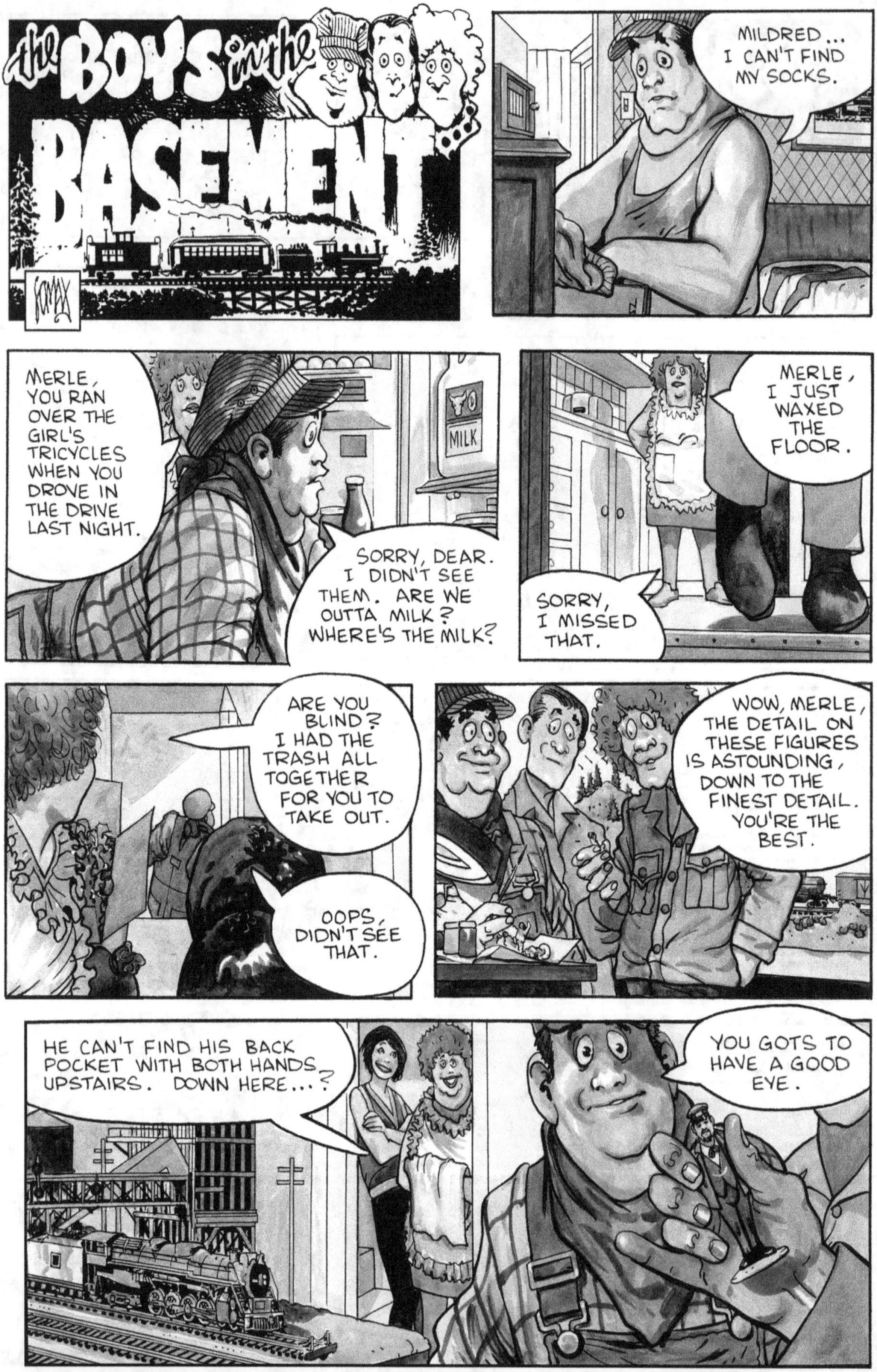
the BOYS in the BASEMENT
MILDRED... I CAN'T FIND MY SOCKS.
MERLE, YOU RAN OVER THE GIRL'S TRICYCLES WHEN YOU DROVE IN THE DRIVE LAST NIGHT.
SORRY, DEAR. I DIDN'T SEE THEM. ARE WE OUTTA MILK? WHERE'S THE MILK?
MILK
MERLE, I JUST WAXED THE FLOOR.
SORRY, I MISSED THAT.
ARE YOU BLIND? I HAD THE TRASH ALL TOGETHER FOR YOU TO TAKE OUT.
OOPS, DIDN'T SEE THAT.
WOW, MERLE, THE DETAIL ON THESE FIGURES IS ASTOUNDING, DOWN TO THE FINEST DETAIL. YOU'RE THE BEST.
HE CAN'T FIND HIS BACK POCKET WITH BOTH HANDS UPSTAIRS. DOWN HERE...?
YOU GOTS TO HAVE A GOOD EYE.

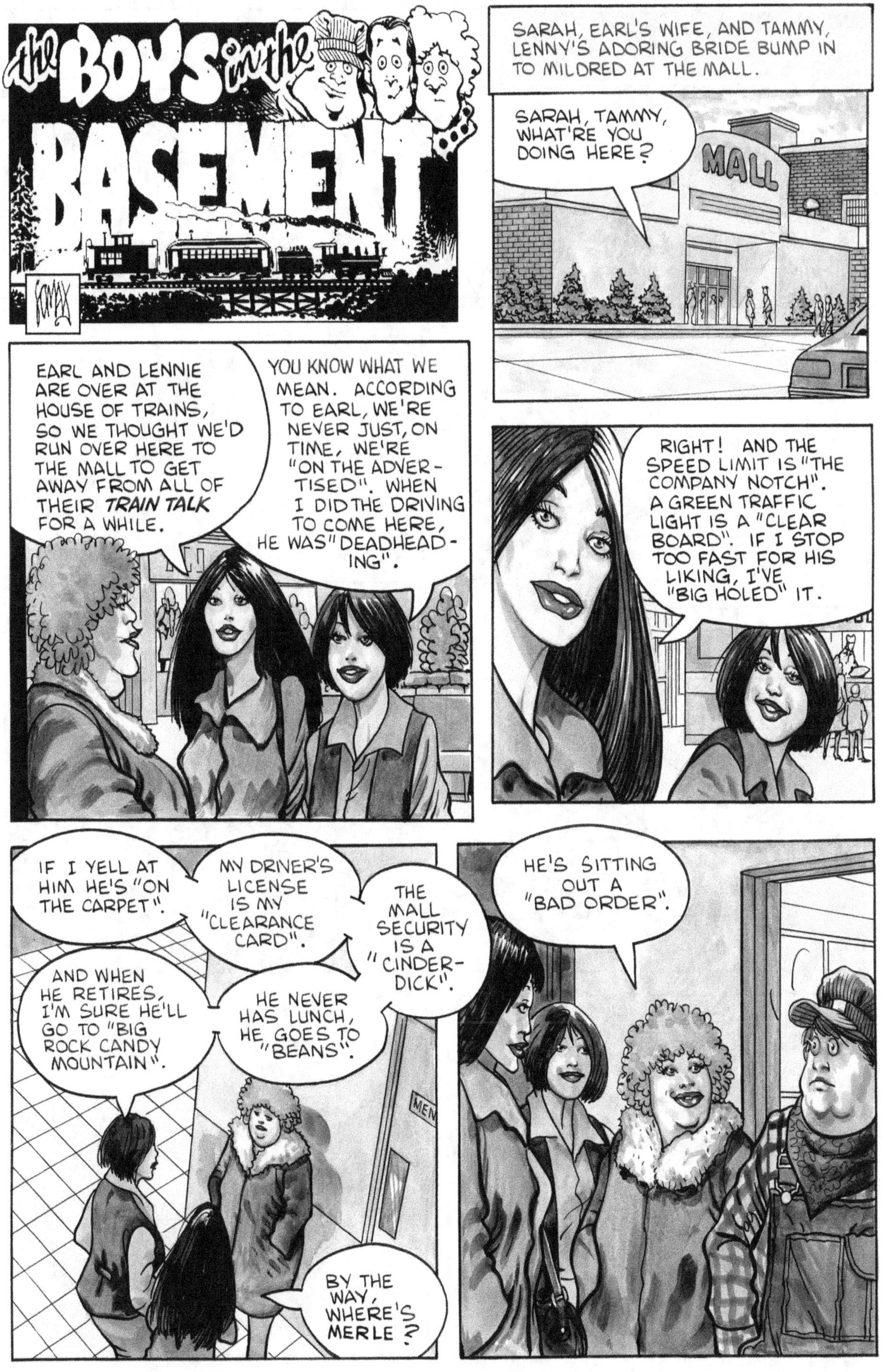
the BOYS in the BASEMENT
SARAH, EARL'S WIFE, AND TAMMY, LENNY'S ADORING BRIDE BUMP IN TO MILDRED AT THE MALL.
SARAH, TAMMY, WHAT'RE YOU DOING HERE?
MALL
EARL AND LENNIE ARE OVER AT THE HOUSE OF TRAINS, SO WE THOUGHT WE'D RUN OVER HERE TO THE MALL TO GET AWAY FROM ALL OF THEIR TRAIN TALK FOR A WHILE.
YOU KNOW WHAT WE MEAN. ACCORDING TO EARL, WE'RE NEVER JUST, ON TIME, WE'RE "ON THE ADVERTISED". WHEN I DID THE DRIVING TO COME HERE, HE WAS "DEADHEADING".
RIGHT! AND THE SPEED LIMIT IS "THE COMPANY NOTCH". A GREEN TRAFFIC LIGHT IS A "CLEAR BOARD". IF I STOP TOO FAST FOR HIS LIKING, I'VE "BIG HOLED" IT.
IF I YELL AT HIM HE'S "ON THE CARPET".
MY DRIVER'S LICENSE IS MY "CLEARANCE CARD".
THE MALL SECURITY IS A "CINDER-DICK".
AND WHEN HE RETIRES, I'M SURE HE'LL GO TO "BIG ROCK CANDY MOUNTAIN".
HE NEVER HAS LUNCH, HE GOES TO "BEANS".
MEN
BY THE WAY, WHERE'S MERLE?
HE'S SITTING OUT A "BAD ORDER".

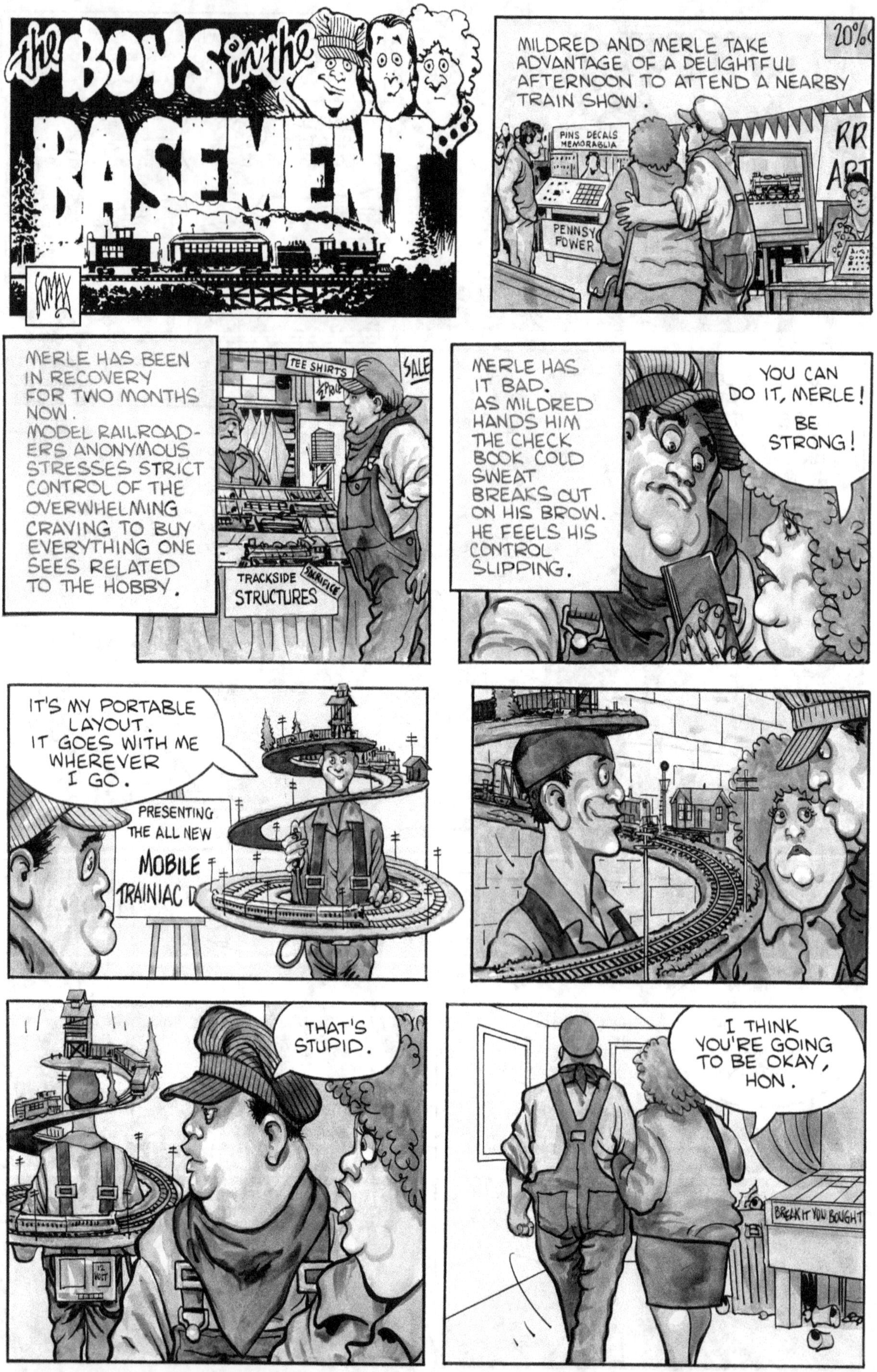
the BOYS in the BASEMENT
SOMAX
MILDRED AND MERLE TAKE ADVANTAGE OF A DELIGHTFUL AFTERNOON TO ATTEND A NEARBY TRAIN SHOW.
20%
PINS DECALS MEMORABILIA
PENNSY POWER
RR ART
MERLE HAS BEEN IN RECOVERY FOR TWO MONTHS NOW. MODEL RAILROADERS ANONYMOUS STRESSES STRICT CONTROL OF THE OVERWHELMING CRAVING TO BUY EVERYTHING ONE SEES RELATED TO THE HOBBY.
TEE SHIRTS
SALE
TRACKSIDE STRUCTURES
SACRIFICE
MERLE HAS IT BAD. AS MILDRED HANDS HIM THE CHECK BOOK COLD SWEAT BREAKS OUT ON HIS BROW. HE FEELS HIS CONTROL SLIPPING.
YOU CAN DO IT, MERLE!
BE STRONG!
IT'S MY PORTABLE LAYOUT. IT GOES WITH ME WHEREVER I GO.
PRESENTING THE ALL NEW MOBILE TRAINIAC D
THAT'S STUPID.
I THINK YOU'RE GOING TO BE OKAY, HON.
BREAK IT YOU BOUGHT

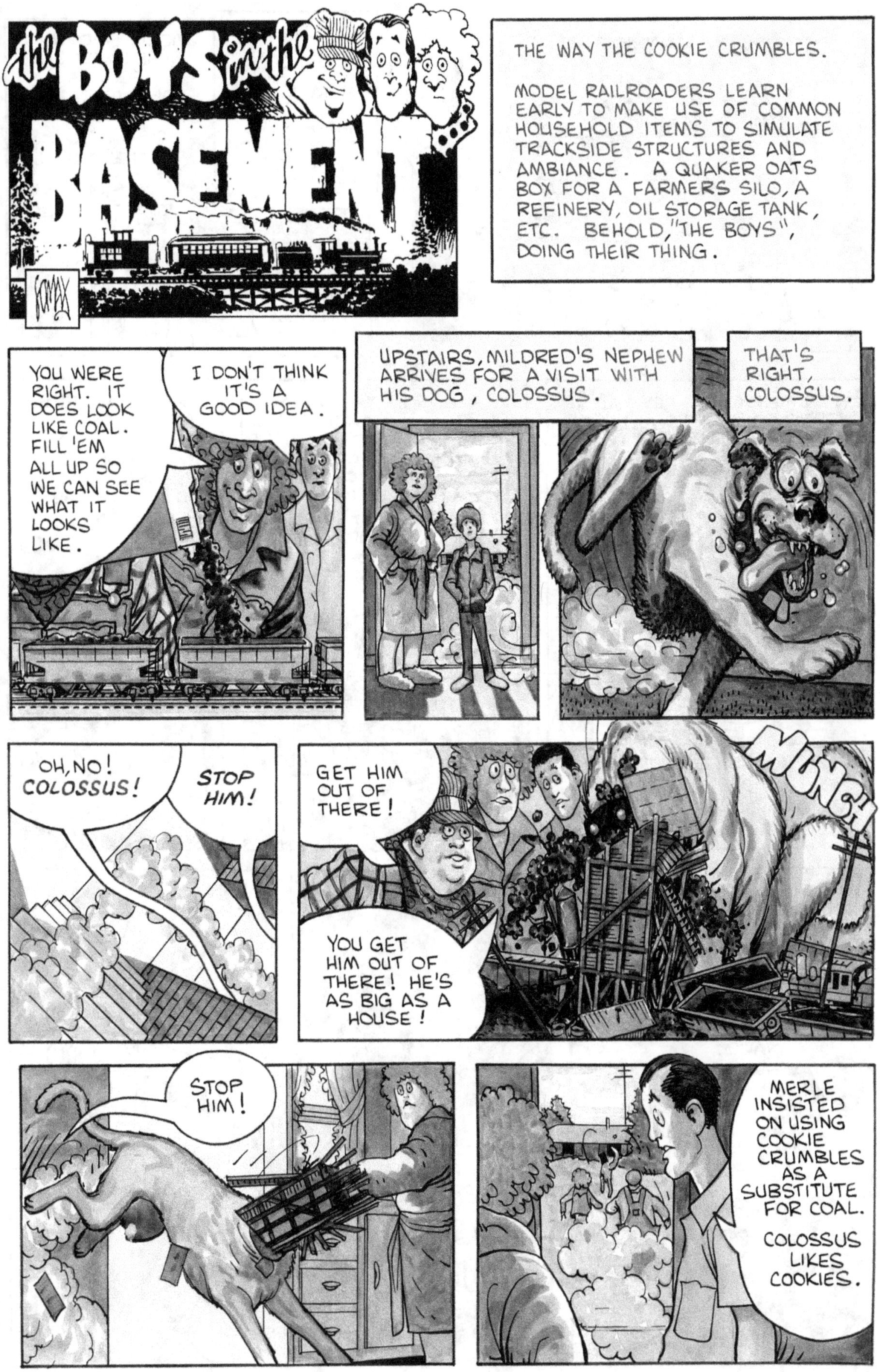
the BOYS in the BASEMENT
THE WAY THE COOKIE CRUMBLES.
MODEL RAILROADERS LEARN EARLY TO MAKE USE OF COMMON HOUSEHOLD ITEMS TO SIMULATE TRACKSIDE STRUCTURES AND AMBIANCE. A QUAKER OATS BOX FOR A FARMERS SILO, A REFINERY, OIL STORAGE TANK, ETC. BEHOLD, "THE BOYS", DOING THEIR THING.
YOU WERE RIGHT. IT DOES LOOK LIKE COAL. FILL 'EM ALL UP SO WE CAN SEE WHAT IT LOOKS LIKE.
I DON'T THINK IT'S A GOOD IDEA.
UPSTAIRS, MILDRED'S NEPHEW ARRIVES FOR A VISIT WITH HIS DOG, COLOSSUS.
THAT'S RIGHT, COLOSSUS.
OH, NO! COLOSSUS!
STOP HIM!
GET HIM OUT OF THERE!
MUNCH
YOU GET HIM OUT OF THERE! HE'S AS BIG AS A HOUSE!
STOP HIM!
MERLE INSISTED ON USING COOKIE CRUMBLES AS A SUBSTITUTE FOR COAL.
COLOSSUS LIKES COOKIES.

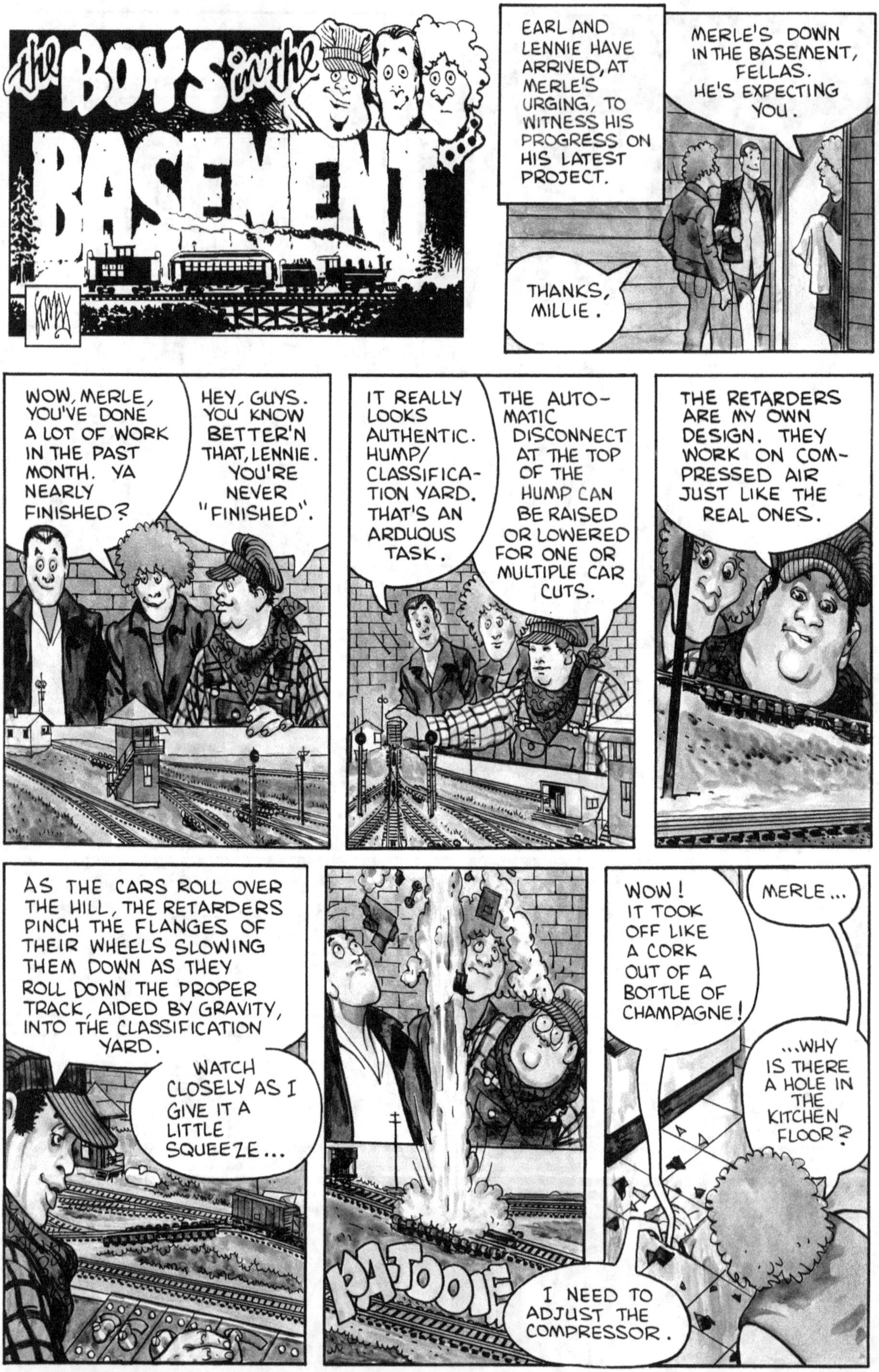
the BOYS in the BASEMENT
EARL AND LENNIE HAVE ARRIVED, AT MERLE'S URGING, TO WITNESS HIS PROGRESS ON HIS LATEST PROJECT.
MERLE'S DOWN IN THE BASEMENT, FELLAS. HE'S EXPECTING YOU.
THANKS, MILLIE.
WOW, MERLE, YOU'VE DONE A LOT OF WORK IN THE PAST MONTH. YA NEARLY FINISHED?
HEY, GUYS. YOU KNOW BETTER'N THAT, LENNIE. YOU'RE NEVER "FINISHED".
IT REALLY LOOKS AUTHENTIC. HUMP/ CLASSIFICATION YARD. THAT'S AN ARDUOUS TASK.
THE AUTOMATIC DISCONNECT AT THE TOP OF THE HUMP CAN BE RAISED OR LOWERED FOR ONE OR MULTIPLE CAR CUTS.
THE RETARDERS ARE MY OWN DESIGN. THEY WORK ON COMPRESSED AIR JUST LIKE THE REAL ONES.
AS THE CARS ROLL OVER THE HILL, THE RETARDERS PINCH THE FLANGES OF THEIR WHEELS SLOWING THEM DOWN AS THEY ROLL DOWN THE PROPER TRACK, AIDED BY GRAVITY, INTO THE CLASSIFICATION YARD.
WATCH CLOSELY AS I GIVE IT A LITTLE SQUEEZE...
PATOOIE
WOW! IT TOOK OFF LIKE A CORK OUT OF A BOTTLE OF CHAMPAGNE!
I NEED TO ADJUST THE COMPRESSOR.
MERLE...
...WHY IS THERE A HOLE IN THE KITCHEN FLOOR?

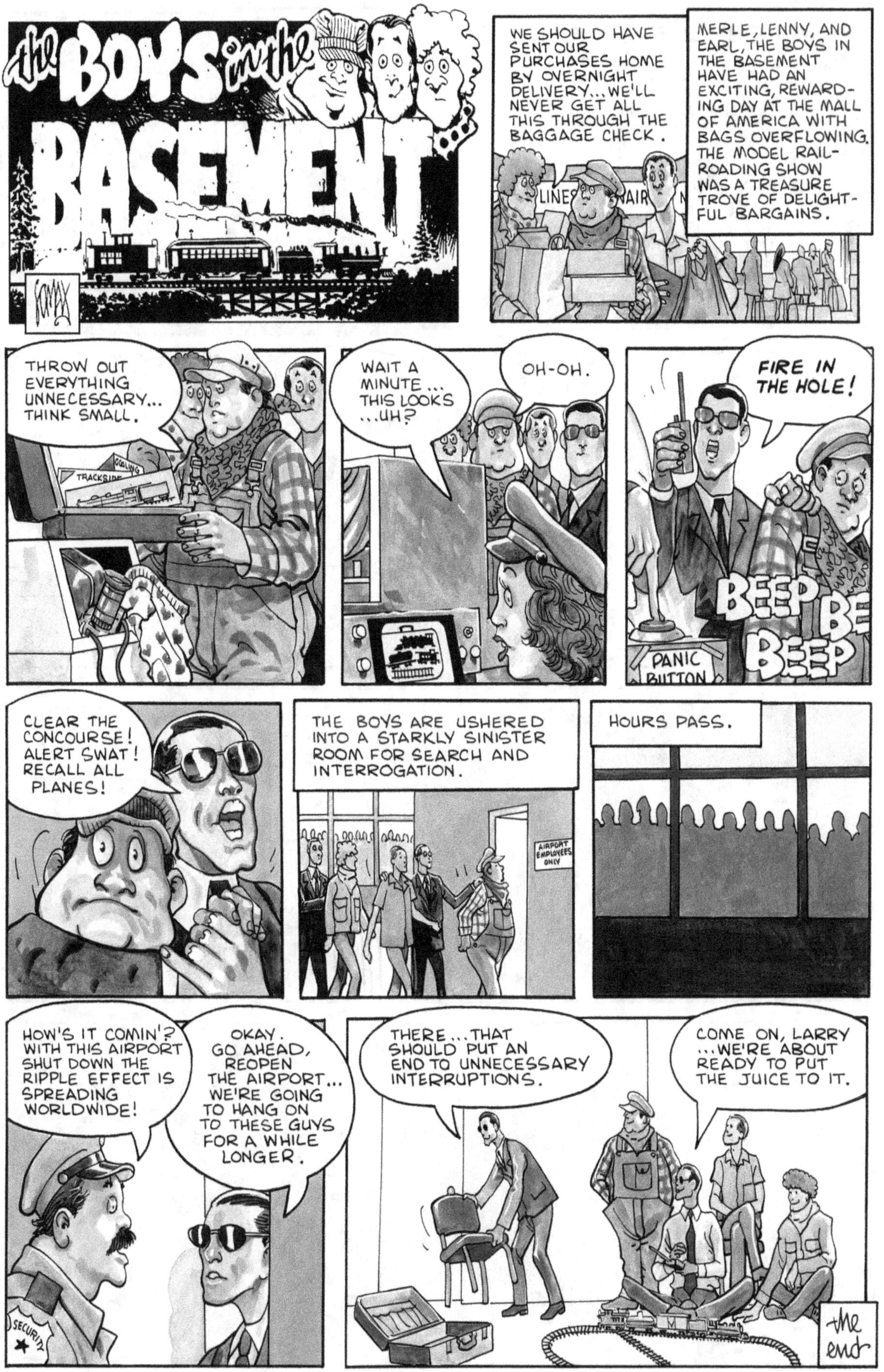
the BOYS in the BASEMENT
WE SHOULD HAVE SENT OUR PURCHASES HOME BY OVERNIGHT DELIVERY... WE'LL NEVER GET ALL THIS THROUGH THE BAGGAGE CHECK.
MERLE, LENNY, AND EARL, THE BOYS IN THE BASEMENT HAVE HAD AN EXCITING, REWARDING DAY AT THE MALL OF AMERICA WITH BAGS OVERFLOWING. THE MODEL RAILROADING SHOW WAS A TREASURE TROVE OF DELIGHTFUL BARGAINS.
THROW OUT EVERYTHING UNNECESSARY... THINK SMALL.
TRACKSIDE
WAIT A MINUTE... THIS LOOKS ...UH?
OH-OH.
FIRE IN THE HOLE!
BEEP BE BEEP
PANIC BUTTON
CLEAR THE CONCOURSE! ALERT SWAT! RECALL ALL PLANES!
THE BOYS ARE USHERED INTO A STARKLY SINISTER ROOM FOR SEARCH AND INTERROGATION.
AIRPORT EMPLOYEES ONLY
HOURS PASS.
HOW'S IT COMIN'? WITH THIS AIRPORT SHUT DOWN THE RIPPLE EFFECT IS SPREADING WORLDWIDE!
OKAY. GO AHEAD, REOPEN THE AIRPORT... WE'RE GOING TO HANG ON TO THESE GUYS FOR A WHILE LONGER.
SECURITY
THERE... THAT SHOULD PUT AN END TO UNNECESSARY INTERRUPTIONS.
COME ON, LARRY ...WE'RE ABOUT READY TO PUT THE JUICE TO IT.
the end

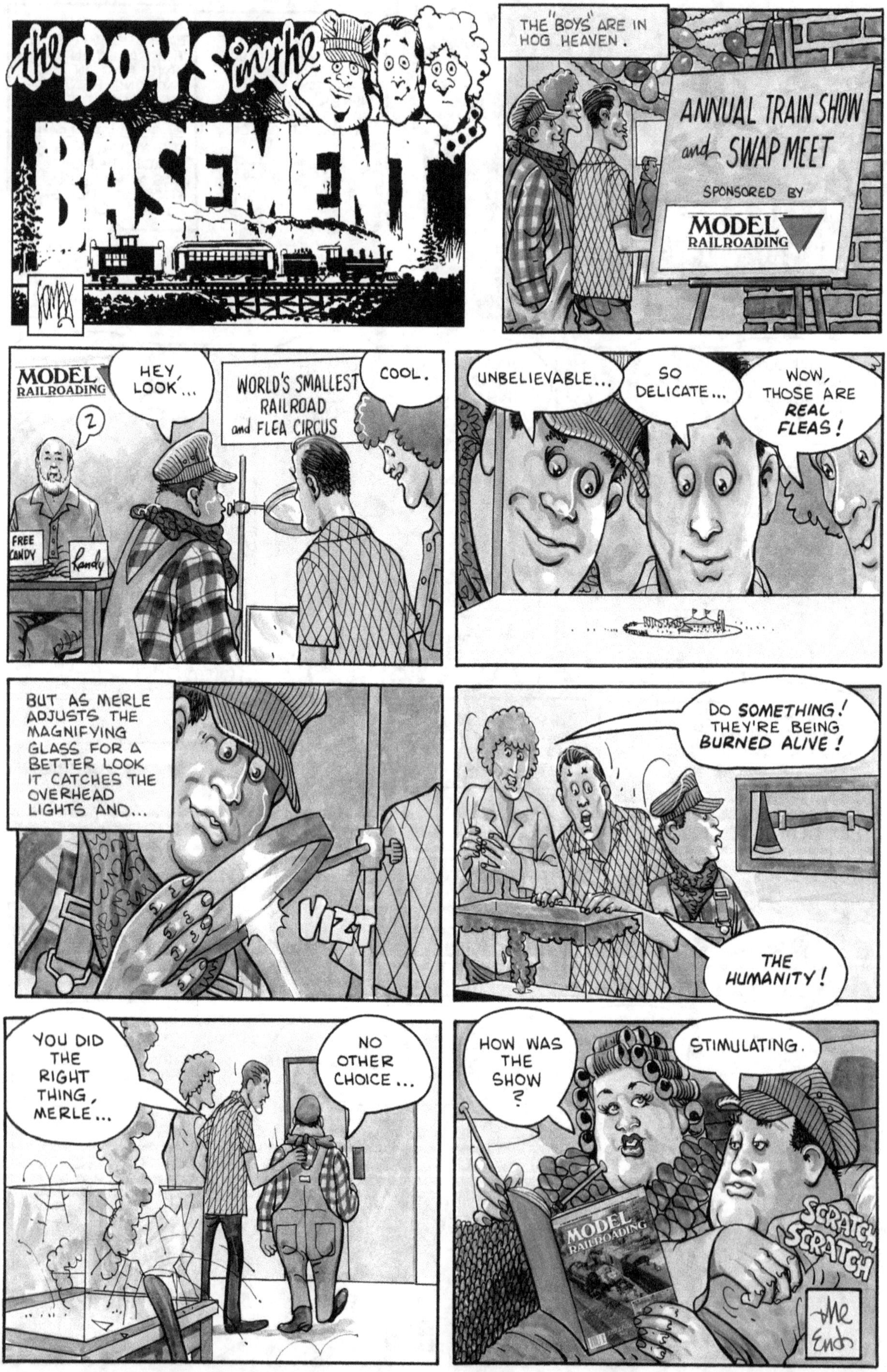
the BOYS in the BASEMENT
THE "BOYS" ARE IN HOG HEAVEN.
ANNUAL TRAIN SHOW and SWAP MEET
SPONSORED BY
MODEL RAILROADING
MODEL RAILROADING
HEY, LOOK...
?
WORLD'S SMALLEST RAILROAD and FLEA CIRCUS
COOL.
FREE CANDY
Randy
UNBELIEVABLE...
SO DELICATE...
WOW, THOSE ARE REAL FLEAS!
BUT AS MERLE ADJUSTS THE MAGNIFYING GLASS FOR A BETTER LOOK IT CATCHES THE OVERHEAD LIGHTS AND...
VIZT
DO SOMETHING! THEY'RE BEING BURNED ALIVE!
THE HUMANITY!
YOU DID THE RIGHT THING, MERLE...
NO OTHER CHOICE...
HOW WAS THE SHOW?
STIMULATING.
MODEL RAILROADING
SCRATCH SCRATCH
the End

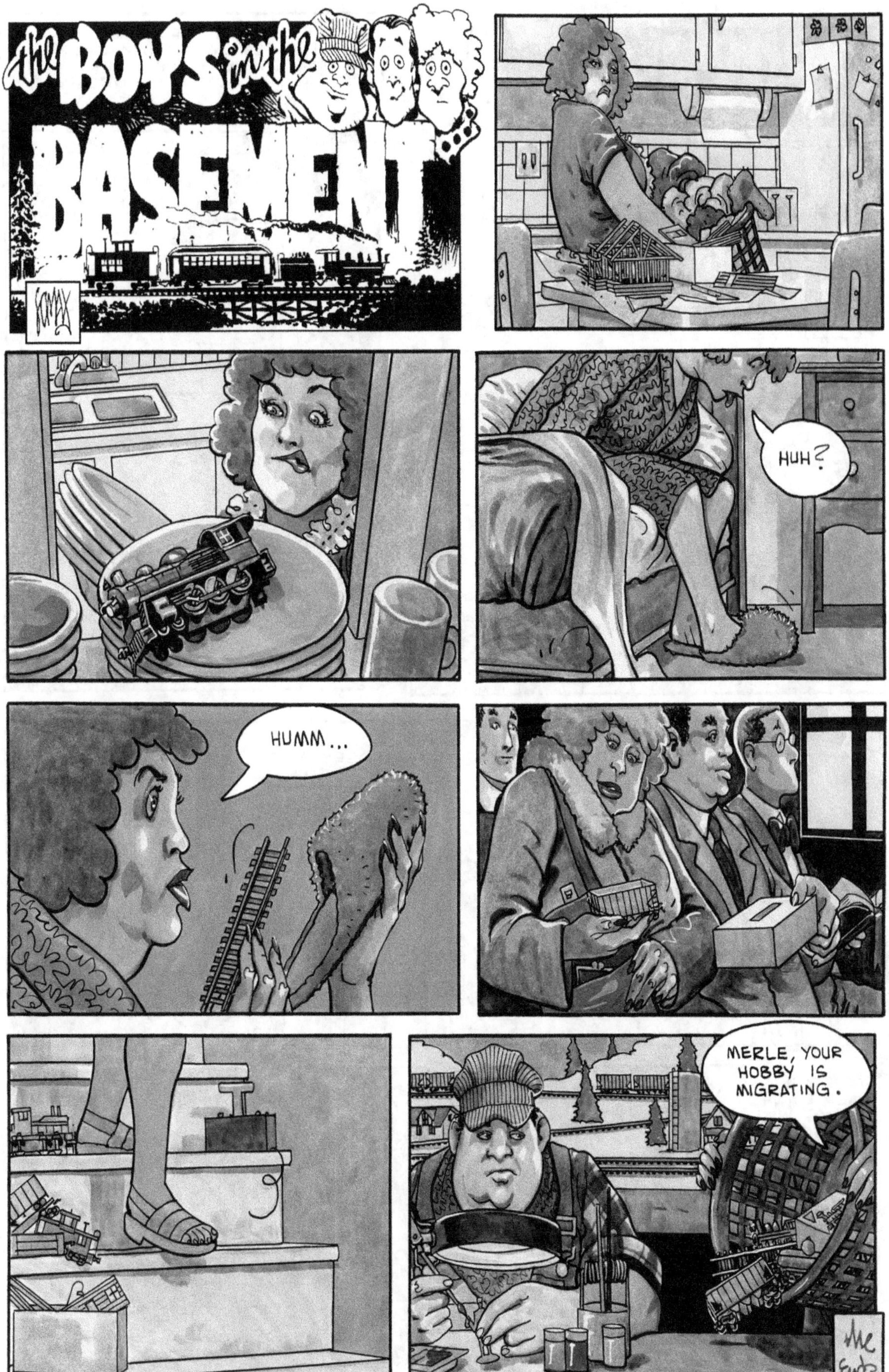
the BOYS in the BASEMENT
HUH?
HUMM...
MERLE, YOUR HOBBY IS MIGRATING.
The End

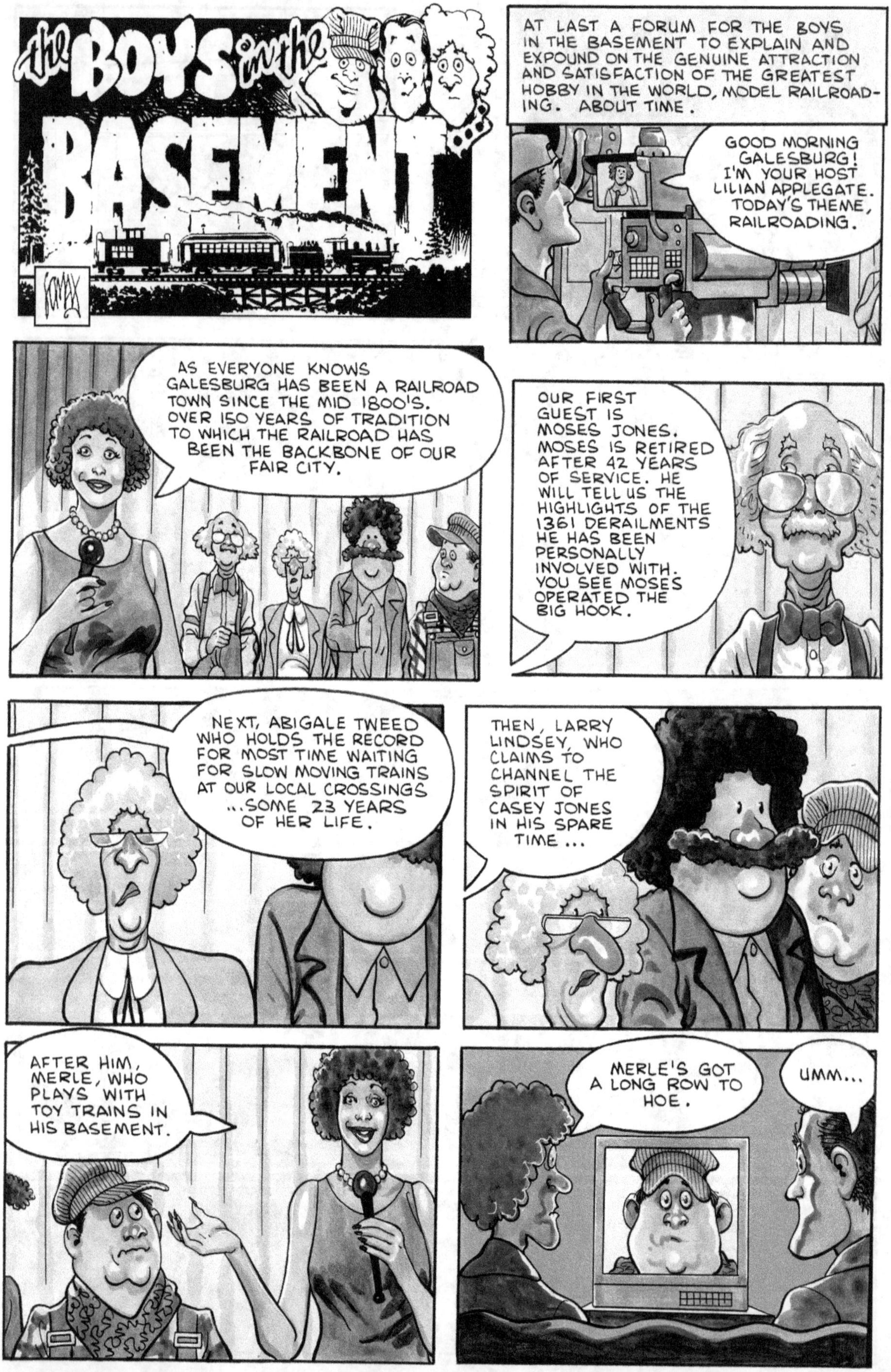
the BOYS in the BASEMENT
AT LAST A FORUM FOR THE BOYS IN THE BASEMENT TO EXPLAIN AND EXPOUND ON THE GENUINE ATTRACTION AND SATISFACTION OF THE GREATEST HOBBY IN THE WORLD, MODEL RAILROADING. ABOUT TIME.
GOOD MORNING GALESBURG! I'M YOUR HOST LILIAN APPLEGATE. TODAY'S THEME, RAILROADING.
AS EVERYONE KNOWS GALESBURG HAS BEEN A RAILROAD TOWN SINCE THE MID 1800'S. OVER 150 YEARS OF TRADITION TO WHICH THE RAILROAD HAS BEEN THE BACKBONE OF OUR FAIR CITY.
OUR FIRST GUEST IS MOSES JONES. MOSES IS RETIRED AFTER 42 YEARS OF SERVICE. HE WILL TELL US THE HIGHLIGHTS OF THE 1361 DERAILMENTS HE HAS BEEN PERSONALLY INVOLVED WITH. YOU SEE MOSES OPERATED THE BIG HOOK.
NEXT, ABIGALE TWEED WHO HOLDS THE RECORD FOR MOST TIME WAITING FOR SLOW MOVING TRAINS AT OUR LOCAL CROSSINGS ...SOME 23 YEARS OF HER LIFE.
THEN, LARRY LINDSEY, WHO CLAIMS TO CHANNEL THE SPIRIT OF CASEY JONES IN HIS SPARE TIME...
AFTER HIM, MERLE, WHO PLAYS WITH TOY TRAINS IN HIS BASEMENT.
MERLE'S GOT A LONG ROW TO HOE.
UMM...

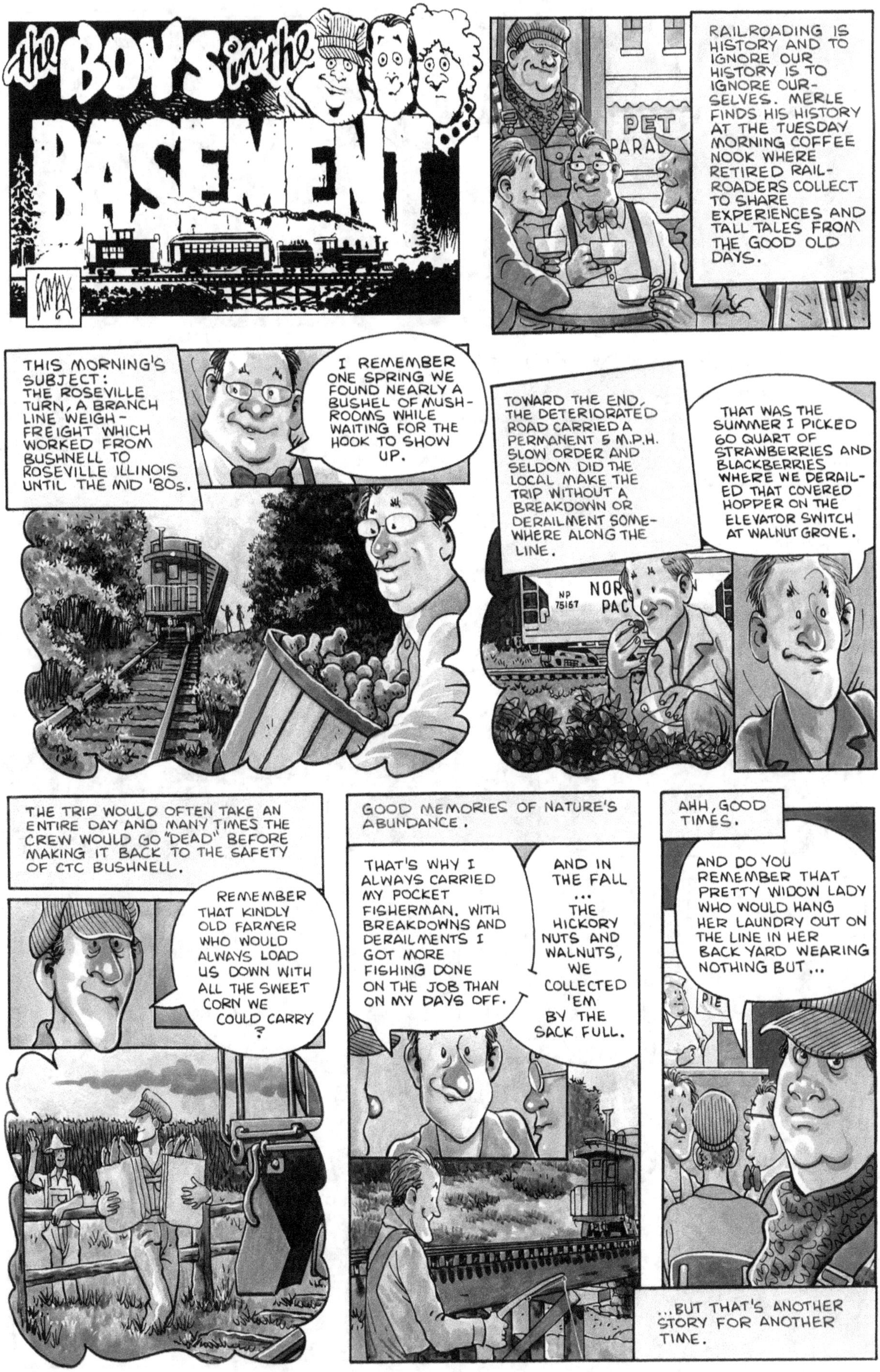
the BOYS in the BASEMENT
SOMAX
RAILROADING IS HISTORY AND TO IGNORE OUR HISTORY IS TO IGNORE OURSELVES. MERLE FINDS HIS HISTORY AT THE TUESDAY MORNING COFFEE NOOK WHERE RETIRED RAILROADERS COLLECT TO SHARE EXPERIENCES AND TALL TALES FROM THE GOOD OLD DAYS.
PET
PARAD
THIS MORNING'S SUBJECT: THE ROSEVILLE TURN, A BRANCH LINE WEIGH-FREIGHT WHICH WORKED FROM BUSHNELL TO ROSEVILLE ILLINOIS UNTIL THE MID '80s.
I REMEMBER ONE SPRING WE FOUND NEARLY A BUSHEL OF MUSHROOMS WHILE WAITING FOR THE HOOK TO SHOW UP.
TOWARD THE END, THE DETERIORATED ROAD CARRIED A PERMANENT 5 M.P.H. SLOW ORDER AND SELDOM DID THE LOCAL MAKE THE TRIP WITHOUT A BREAKDOWN OR DERAILMENT SOMEWHERE ALONG THE LINE.
THAT WAS THE SUMMER I PICKED 60 QUART OF STRAWBERRIES AND BLACKBERRIES WHERE WE DERAILED THAT COVERED HOPPER ON THE ELEVATOR SWITCH AT WALNUT GROVE.
NP 75157
NOR
PAC
THE TRIP WOULD OFTEN TAKE AN ENTIRE DAY AND MANY TIMES THE CREW WOULD GO "DEAD" BEFORE MAKING IT BACK TO THE SAFETY OF CTC BUSHNELL.
REMEMBER THAT KINDLY OLD FARMER WHO WOULD ALWAYS LOAD US DOWN WITH ALL THE SWEET CORN WE COULD CARRY?
GOOD MEMORIES OF NATURE'S ABUNDANCE.
THAT'S WHY I ALWAYS CARRIED MY POCKET FISHERMAN. WITH BREAKDOWNS AND DERAILMENTS I GOT MORE FISHING DONE ON THE JOB THAN ON MY DAYS OFF.
AND IN THE FALL ... THE HICKORY NUTS AND WALNUTS, WE COLLECTED 'EM BY THE SACK FULL.
AHH, GOOD TIMES.
AND DO YOU REMEMBER THAT PRETTY WIDOW LADY WHO WOULD HANG HER LAUNDRY OUT ON THE LINE IN HER BACK YARD WEARING NOTHING BUT...
PIE
...BUT THAT'S ANOTHER STORY FOR ANOTHER TIME.

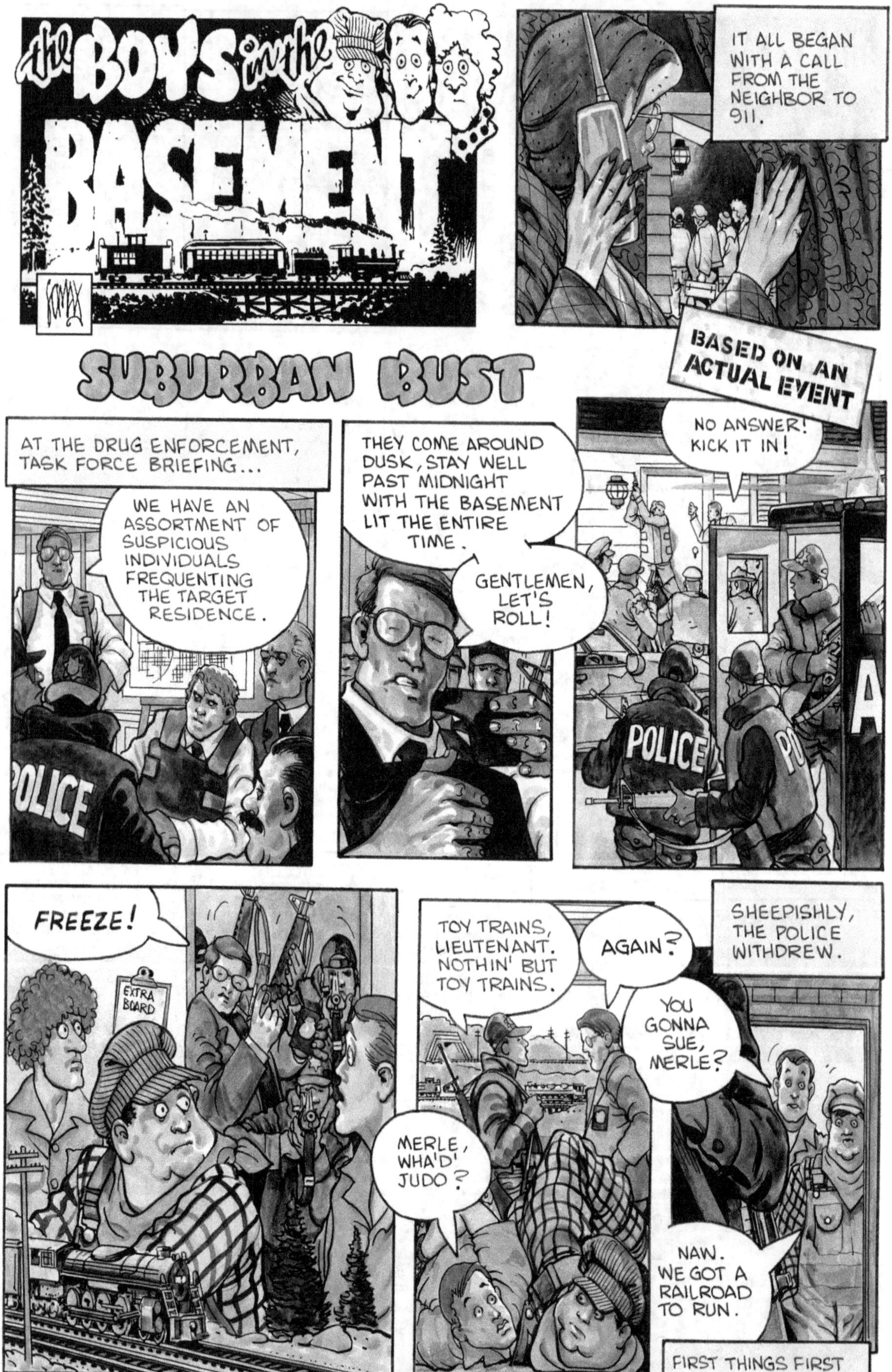
the BOYS in the BASEMENT
IT ALL BEGAN WITH A CALL FROM THE NEIGHBOR TO 911.
SUBURBAN BUST
BASED ON AN ACTUAL EVENT
AT THE DRUG ENFORCEMENT, TASK FORCE BRIEFING...
WE HAVE AN ASSORTMENT OF SUSPICIOUS INDIVIDUALS FREQUENTING THE TARGET RESIDENCE.
POLICE
THEY COME AROUND DUSK, STAY WELL PAST MIDNIGHT WITH THE BASEMENT LIT THE ENTIRE TIME.
GENTLEMEN, LET'S ROLL!
NO ANSWER! KICK IT IN!
POLICE
FREEZE!
EXTRA BOARD
TOY TRAINS, LIEUTENANT. NOTHIN' BUT TOY TRAINS.
AGAIN?
MERLE, WHA'D' JUDO?
SHEEPISHLY, THE POLICE WITHDREW.
YOU GONNA SUE, MERLE?
NAW. WE GOT A RAILROAD TO RUN.
FIRST THINGS FIRST

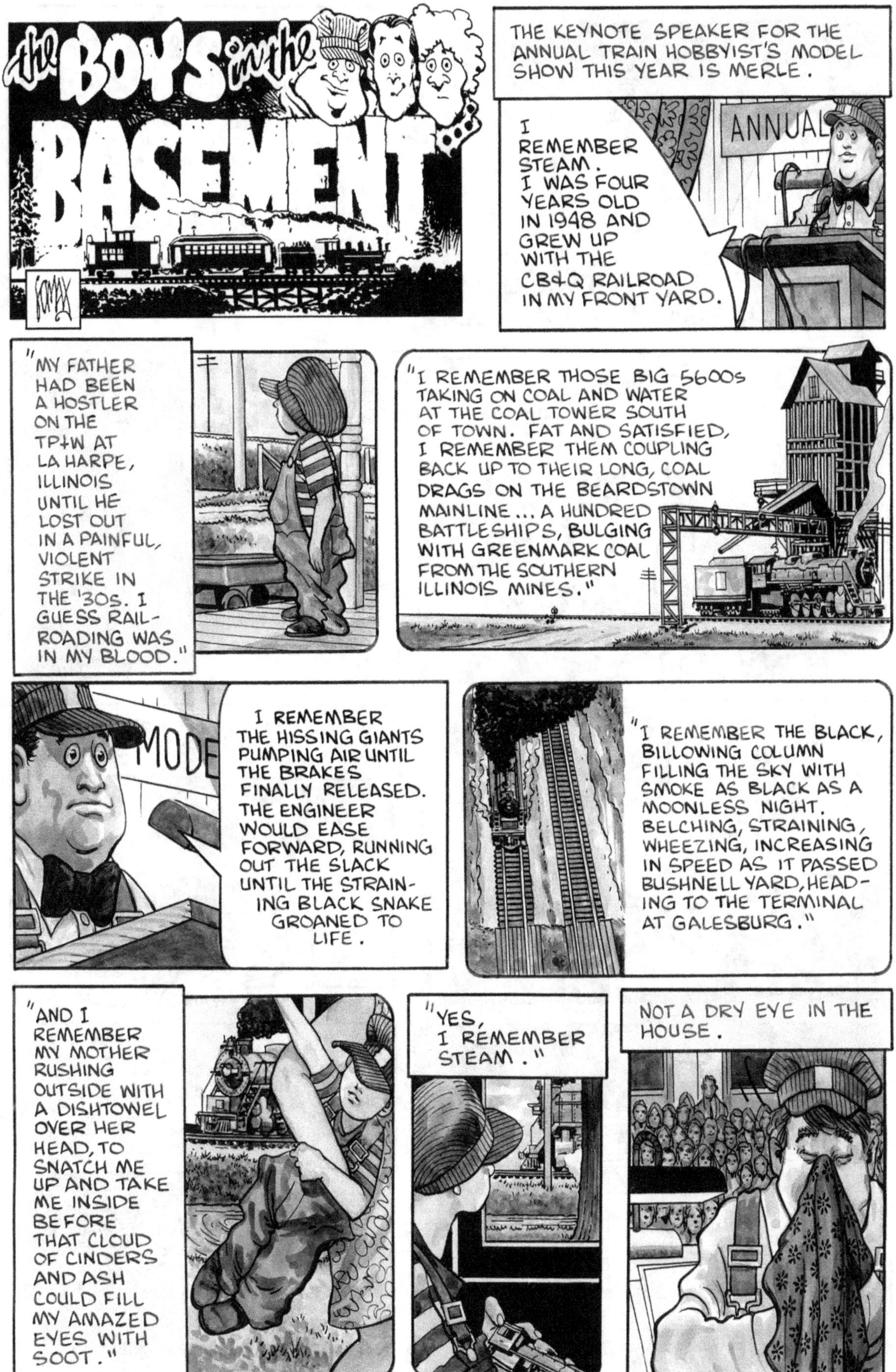
the BOYS in the BASEMENT
THE KEYNOTE SPEAKER FOR THE ANNUAL TRAIN HOBBYIST'S MODEL SHOW THIS YEAR IS MERLE.
ANNUAL
I REMEMBER STEAM. I WAS FOUR YEARS OLD IN 1948 AND GREW UP WITH THE CB&Q RAILROAD IN MY FRONT YARD.
"MY FATHER HAD BEEN A HOSTLER ON THE TP&W AT LA HARPE, ILLINOIS UNTIL HE LOST OUT IN A PAINFUL, VIOLENT STRIKE IN THE '30s. I GUESS RAIL-ROADING WAS IN MY BLOOD."
"I REMEMBER THOSE BIG 5600s TAKING ON COAL AND WATER AT THE COAL TOWER SOUTH OF TOWN. FAT AND SATISFIED, I REMEMBER THEM COUPLING BACK UP TO THEIR LONG, COAL DRAGS ON THE BEARDSTOWN MAINLINE... A HUNDRED BATTLESHIPS, BULGING WITH GREENMARK COAL FROM THE SOUTHERN ILLINOIS MINES."
MODE
I REMEMBER THE HISSING GIANTS PUMPING AIR UNTIL THE BRAKES FINALLY RELEASED. THE ENGINEER WOULD EASE FORWARD, RUNNING OUT THE SLACK UNTIL THE STRAIN-ING BLACK SNAKE GROANED TO LIFE.
"I REMEMBER THE BLACK, BILLOWING COLUMN FILLING THE SKY WITH SMOKE AS BLACK AS A MOONLESS NIGHT. BELCHING, STRAINING, WHEEZING, INCREASING IN SPEED AS IT PASSED BUSHNELL YARD, HEAD-ING TO THE TERMINAL AT GALESBURG."
"AND I REMEMBER MY MOTHER RUSHING OUTSIDE WITH A DISHTOWEL OVER HER HEAD, TO SNATCH ME UP AND TAKE ME INSIDE BEFORE THAT CLOUD OF CINDERS AND ASH COULD FILL MY AMAZED EYES WITH SOOT."
"YES, I REMEMBER STEAM."
NOT A DRY EYE IN THE HOUSE.

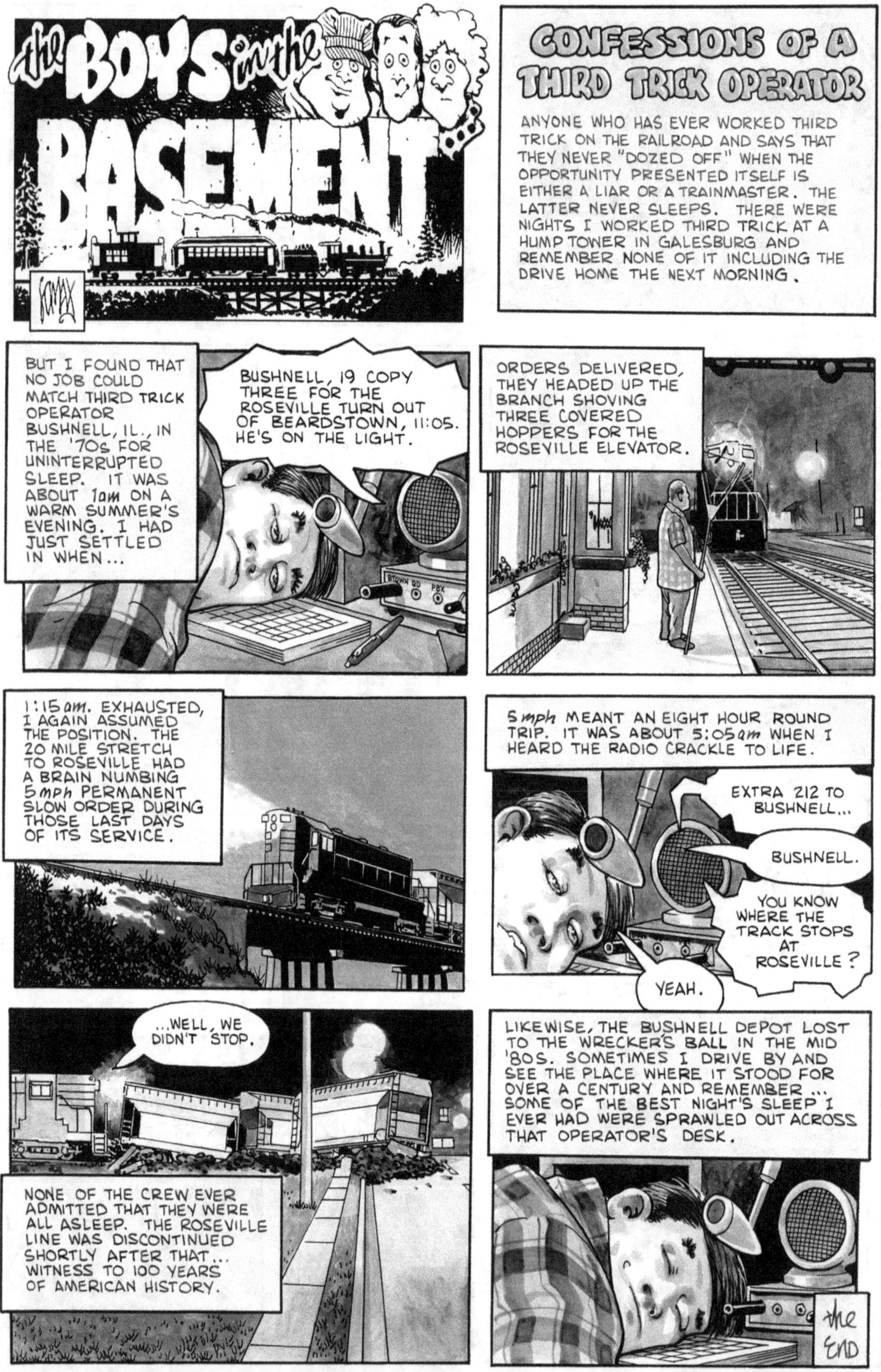

the BOYS in the BASEMENT
CONFESSIONS OF A THIRD TRICK OPERATOR
ANYONE WHO HAS EVER WORKED THIRD TRICK ON THE RAILROAD AND SAYS THAT THEY NEVER "DOZED OFF" WHEN THE OPPORTUNITY PRESENTED ITSELF IS EITHER A LIAR OR A TRAINMASTER. THE LATTER NEVER SLEEPS. THERE WERE NIGHTS I WORKED THIRD TRICK AT A HUMP TOWER IN GALESBURG AND REMEMBER NONE OF IT INCLUDING THE DRIVE HOME THE NEXT MORNING.
BUT I FOUND THAT NO JOB COULD MATCH THIRD TRICK OPERATOR BUSHNELL, IL., IN THE '70s FOR UNINTERRUPTED SLEEP. IT WAS ABOUT 1am ON A WARM SUMMER'S EVENING. I HAD JUST SETTLED IN WHEN...
BUSHNELL, 19 COPY THREE FOR THE ROSEVILLE TURN OUT OF BEARDSTOWN, 11:05. HE'S ON THE LIGHT.
ORDERS DELIVERED, THEY HEADED UP THE BRANCH SHOVING THREE COVERED HOPPERS FOR THE ROSEVILLE ELEVATOR.
1:15am. EXHAUSTED, I AGAIN ASSUMED THE POSITION. THE 20 MILE STRETCH TO ROSEVILLE HAD A BRAIN NUMBING 5mph PERMANENT SLOW ORDER DURING THOSE LAST DAYS OF ITS SERVICE.
5mph MEANT AN EIGHT HOUR ROUND TRIP. IT WAS ABOUT 5:05am WHEN I HEARD THE RADIO CRACKLE TO LIFE.
EXTRA 212 TO BUSHNELL...
BUSHNELL.
YOU KNOW WHERE THE TRACK STOPS AT ROSEVILLE?
YEAH.
...WELL, WE DIDN'T STOP.
NONE OF THE CREW EVER ADMITTED THAT THEY WERE ALL ASLEEP. THE ROSEVILLE LINE WAS DISCONTINUED SHORTLY AFTER THAT... WITNESS TO 100 YEARS OF AMERICAN HISTORY.
LIKEWISE, THE BUSHNELL DEPOT LOST TO THE WRECKER'S BALL IN THE MID '80S. SOMETIMES I DRIVE BY AND SEE THE PLACE WHERE IT STOOD FOR OVER A CENTURY AND REMEMBER... SOME OF THE BEST NIGHT'S SLEEP I EVER HAD WERE SPRAWLED OUT ACROSS THAT OPERATOR'S DESK.
the END

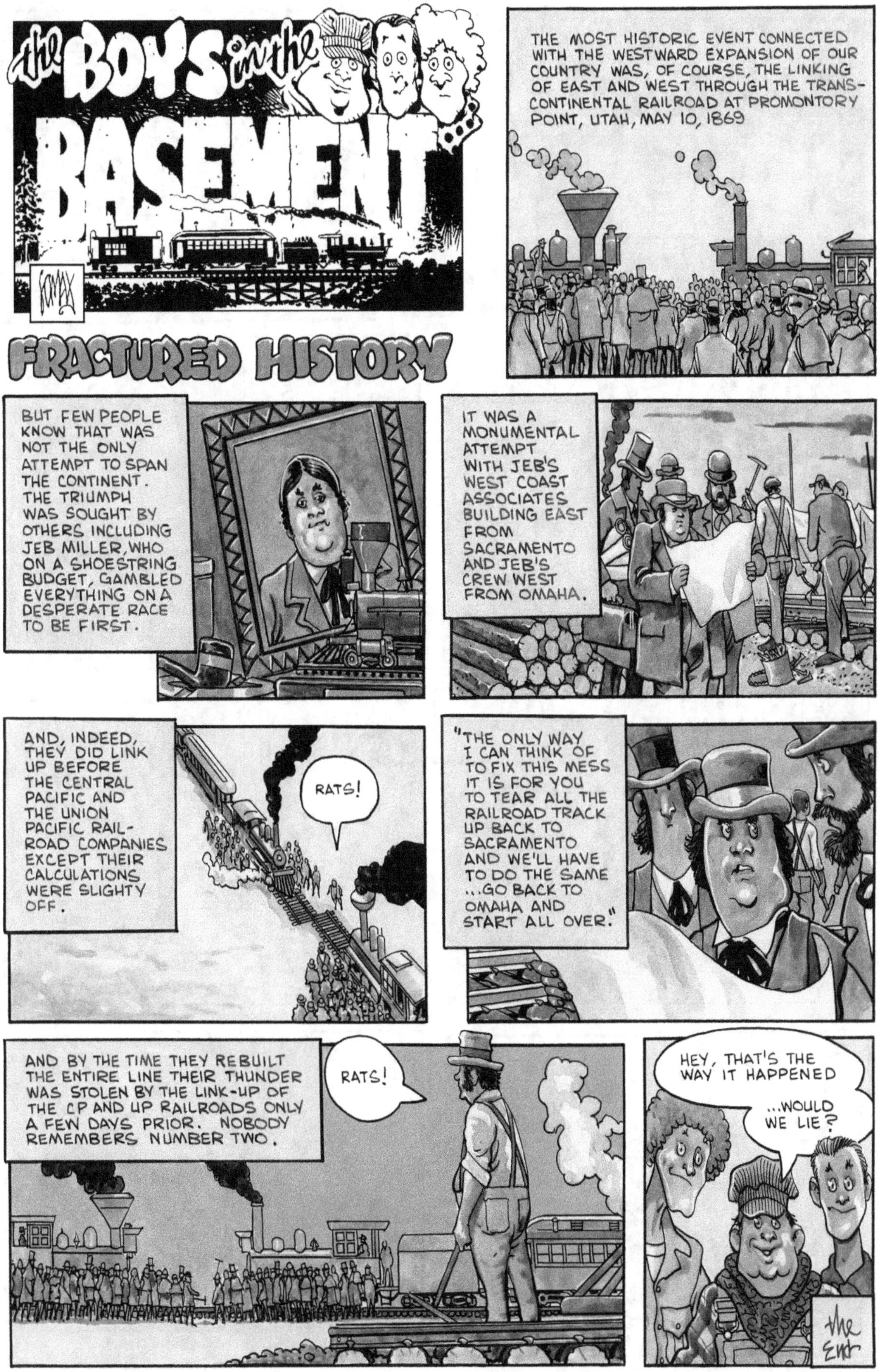
the BOYS in the BASEMENT
FRACTURED HISTORY
THE MOST HISTORIC EVENT CONNECTED WITH THE WESTWARD EXPANSION OF OUR COUNTRY WAS, OF COURSE, THE LINKING OF EAST AND WEST THROUGH THE TRANS-CONTINENTAL RAILROAD AT PROMONTORY POINT, UTAH, MAY 10, 1869
BUT FEW PEOPLE KNOW THAT WAS NOT THE ONLY ATTEMPT TO SPAN THE CONTINENT. THE TRIUMPH WAS SOUGHT BY OTHERS INCLUDING JEB MILLER, WHO ON A SHOESTRING BUDGET, GAMBLED EVERYTHING ON A DESPERATE RACE TO BE FIRST.
IT WAS A MONUMENTAL ATTEMPT WITH JEB'S WEST COAST ASSOCIATES BUILDING EAST FROM SACRAMENTO AND JEB'S CREW WEST FROM OMAHA.
AND, INDEED, THEY DID LINK UP BEFORE THE CENTRAL PACIFIC AND THE UNION PACIFIC RAIL-ROAD COMPANIES EXCEPT THEIR CALCULATIONS WERE SLIGHTY OFF.
RATS!
"THE ONLY WAY I CAN THINK OF TO FIX THIS MESS IT IS FOR YOU TO TEAR ALL THE RAILROAD TRACK UP BACK TO SACRAMENTO AND WE'LL HAVE TO DO THE SAME ...GO BACK TO OMAHA AND START ALL OVER."
AND BY THE TIME THEY REBUILT THE ENTIRE LINE THEIR THUNDER WAS STOLEN BY THE LINK-UP OF THE CP AND UP RAILROADS ONLY A FEW DAYS PRIOR. NOBODY REMEMBERS NUMBER TWO.
RATS!
HEY, THAT'S THE WAY IT HAPPENED
...WOULD WE LIE?
the End

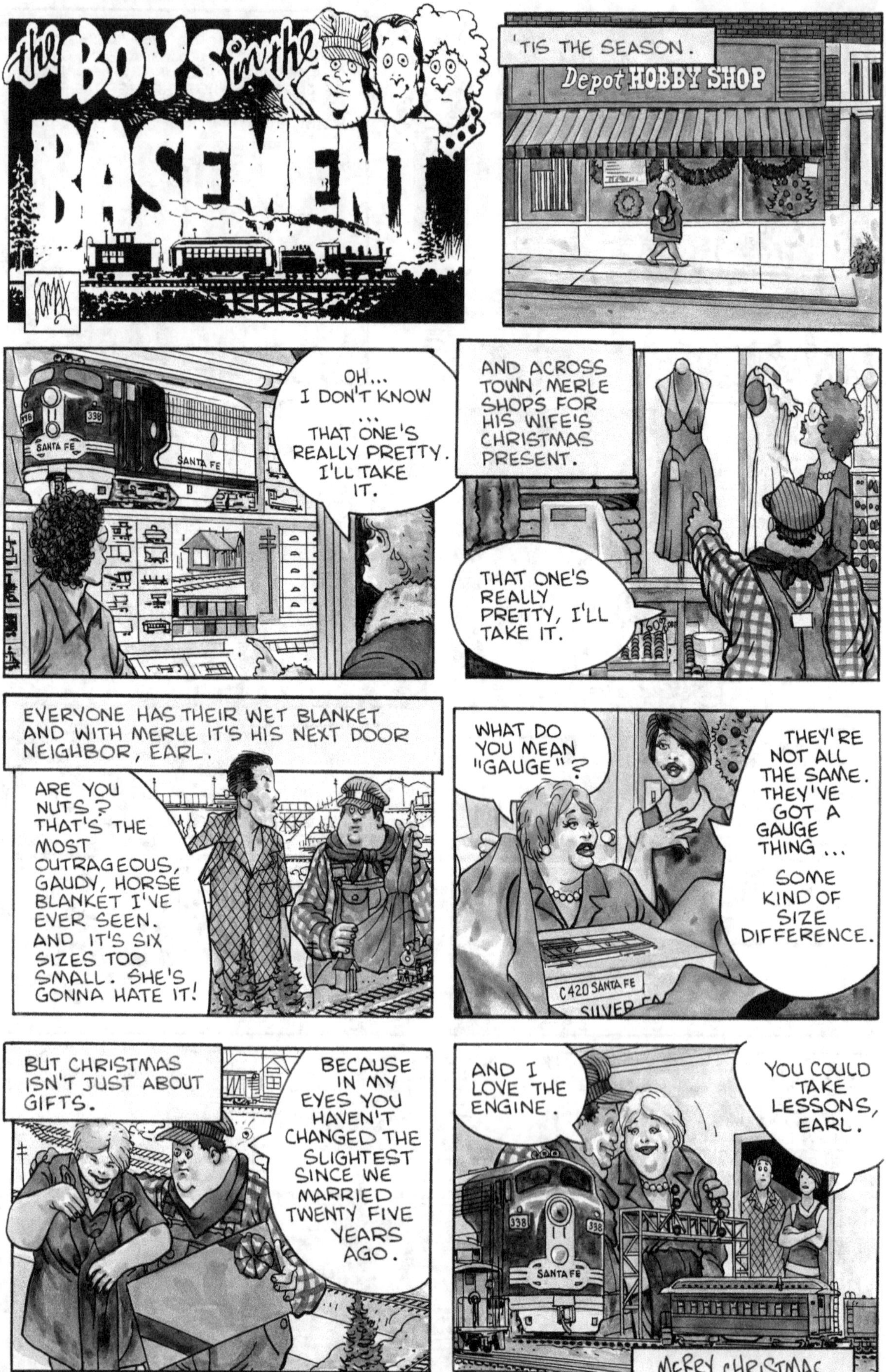
the BOYS in the BASEMENT
'TIS THE SEASON.
Depot HOBBY SHOP
SANTA FE
OH... I DON'T KNOW ... THAT ONE'S REALLY PRETTY. I'LL TAKE IT.
AND ACROSS TOWN, MERLE SHOPS FOR HIS WIFE'S CHRISTMAS PRESENT.
THAT ONE'S REALLY PRETTY, I'LL TAKE IT.
EVERYONE HAS THEIR WET BLANKET AND WITH MERLE IT'S HIS NEXT DOOR NEIGHBOR, EARL.
ARE YOU NUTS? THAT'S THE MOST OUTRAGEOUS, GAUDY, HORSE BLANKET I'VE EVER SEEN. AND IT'S SIX SIZES TOO SMALL. SHE'S GONNA HATE IT!
WHAT DO YOU MEAN "GAUGE"?
THEY'RE NOT ALL THE SAME. THEY'VE GOT A GAUGE THING ...
SOME KIND OF SIZE DIFFERENCE.
C420 SANTA FE
BUT CHRISTMAS ISN'T JUST ABOUT GIFTS.
BECAUSE IN MY EYES YOU HAVEN'T CHANGED THE SLIGHTEST SINCE WE MARRIED TWENTY FIVE YEARS AGO.
AND I LOVE THE ENGINE.
YOU COULD TAKE LESSONS, EARL.
SANTA FE
MERRY CHRISTMAS

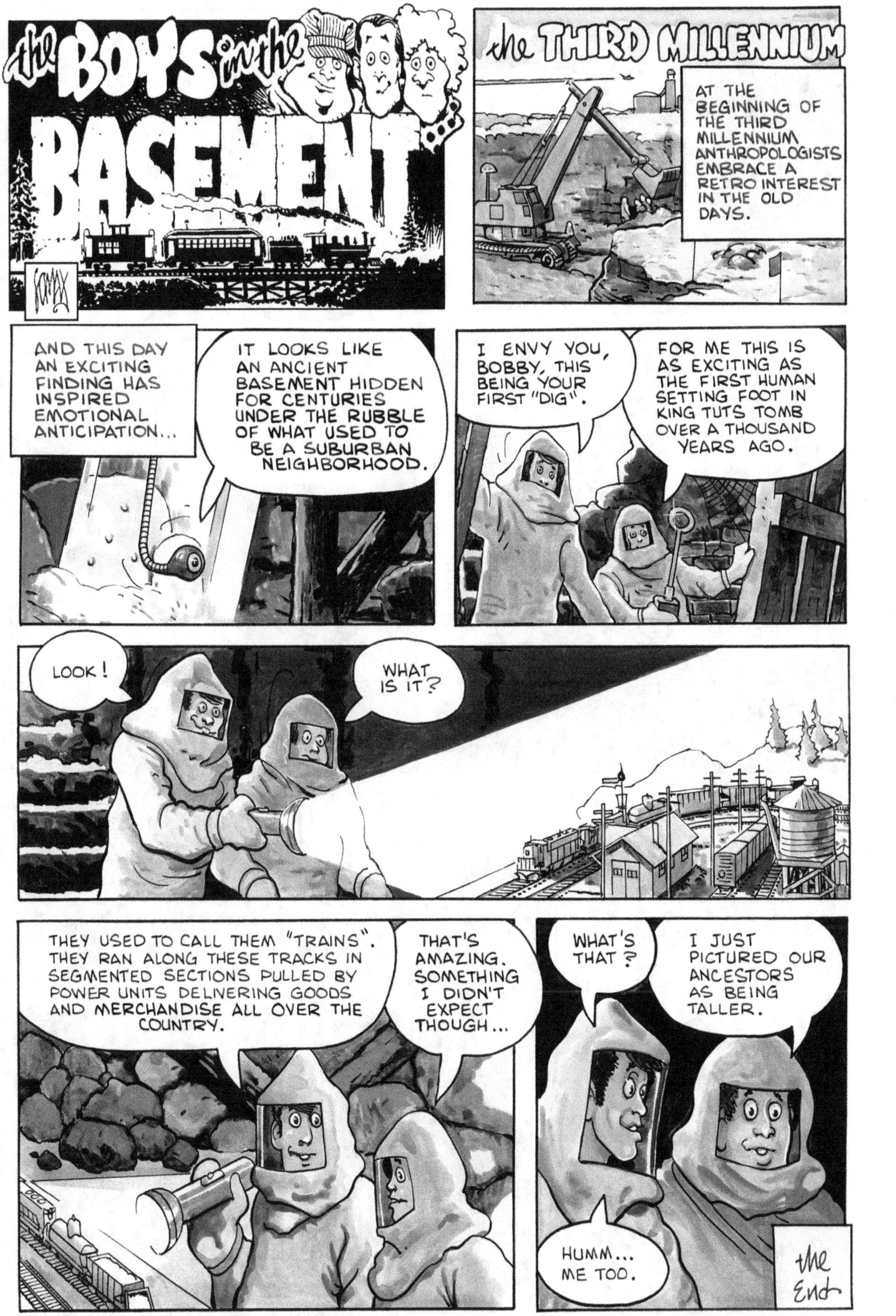

the BOYS in the BASEMENT
the THIRD MILLENNIUM
AT THE BEGINNING OF THE THIRD MILLENNIUM ANTHROPOLOGISTS EMBRACE A RETRO INTEREST IN THE OLD DAYS.
AND THIS DAY AN EXCITING FINDING HAS INSPIRED EMOTIONAL ANTICIPATION...
IT LOOKS LIKE AN ANCIENT BASEMENT HIDDEN FOR CENTURIES UNDER THE RUBBLE OF WHAT USED TO BE A SUBURBAN NEIGHBORHOOD.
I ENVY YOU, BOBBY, THIS BEING YOUR FIRST "DIG".
FOR ME THIS IS AS EXCITING AS THE FIRST HUMAN SETTING FOOT IN KING TUTS TOMB OVER A THOUSAND YEARS AGO.
LOOK!
WHAT IS IT?
THEY USED TO CALL THEM "TRAINS". THEY RAN ALONG THESE TRACKS IN SEGMENTED SECTIONS PULLED BY POWER UNITS DELIVERING GOODS AND MERCHANDISE ALL OVER THE COUNTRY.
THAT'S AMAZING. SOMETHING I DIDN'T EXPECT THOUGH...
WHAT'S THAT?
I JUST PICTURED OUR ANCESTORS AS BEING TALLER.
HUMM... ME TOO.
the End

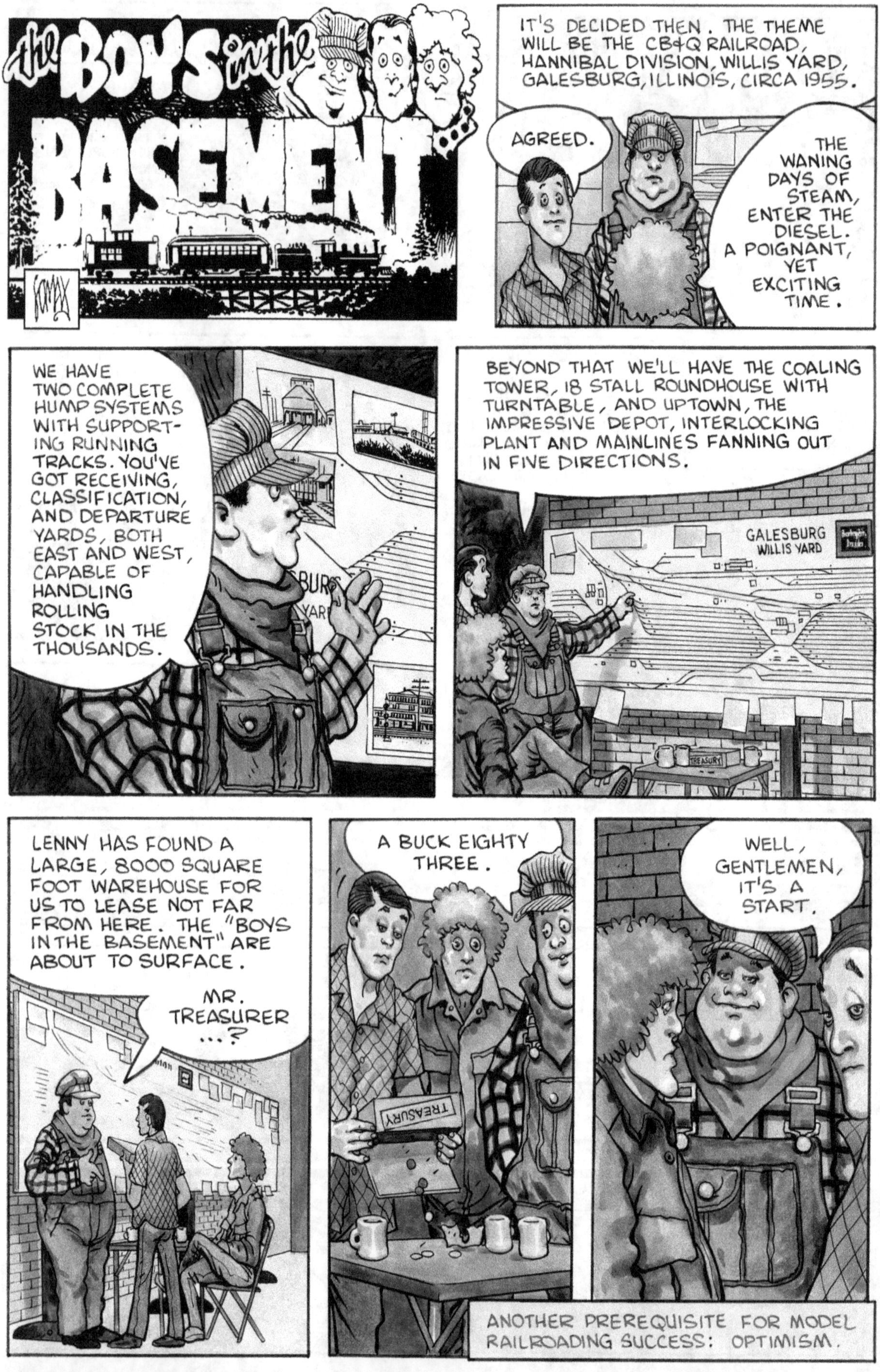
the BOYS in the BASEMENT
IT'S DECIDED THEN. THE THEME WILL BE THE CB&Q RAILROAD, HANNIBAL DIVISION, WILLIS YARD, GALESBURG, ILLINOIS, CIRCA 1955.
AGREED.
THE WANING DAYS OF STEAM, ENTER THE DIESEL. A POIGNANT, YET EXCITING TIME.
WE HAVE TWO COMPLETE HUMP SYSTEMS WITH SUPPORTING RUNNING TRACKS. YOU'VE GOT RECEIVING, CLASSIFICATION, AND DEPARTURE YARDS, BOTH EAST AND WEST, CAPABLE OF HANDLING ROLLING STOCK IN THE THOUSANDS.
BEYOND THAT WE'LL HAVE THE COALING TOWER, 18 STALL ROUNDHOUSE WITH TURNTABLE, AND UPTOWN, THE IMPRESSIVE DEPOT, INTERLOCKING PLANT AND MAINLINES FANNING OUT IN FIVE DIRECTIONS.
GALESBURG
WILLIS YARD
TREASURY
LENNY HAS FOUND A LARGE, 8000 SQUARE FOOT WAREHOUSE FOR US TO LEASE NOT FAR FROM HERE. THE "BOYS IN THE BASEMENT" ARE ABOUT TO SURFACE.
MR. TREASURER ...?
A BUCK EIGHTY THREE.
TREASURY
WELL, GENTLEMEN, IT'S A START.
ANOTHER PREREQUISITE FOR MODEL RAILROADING SUCCESS: OPTIMISM.

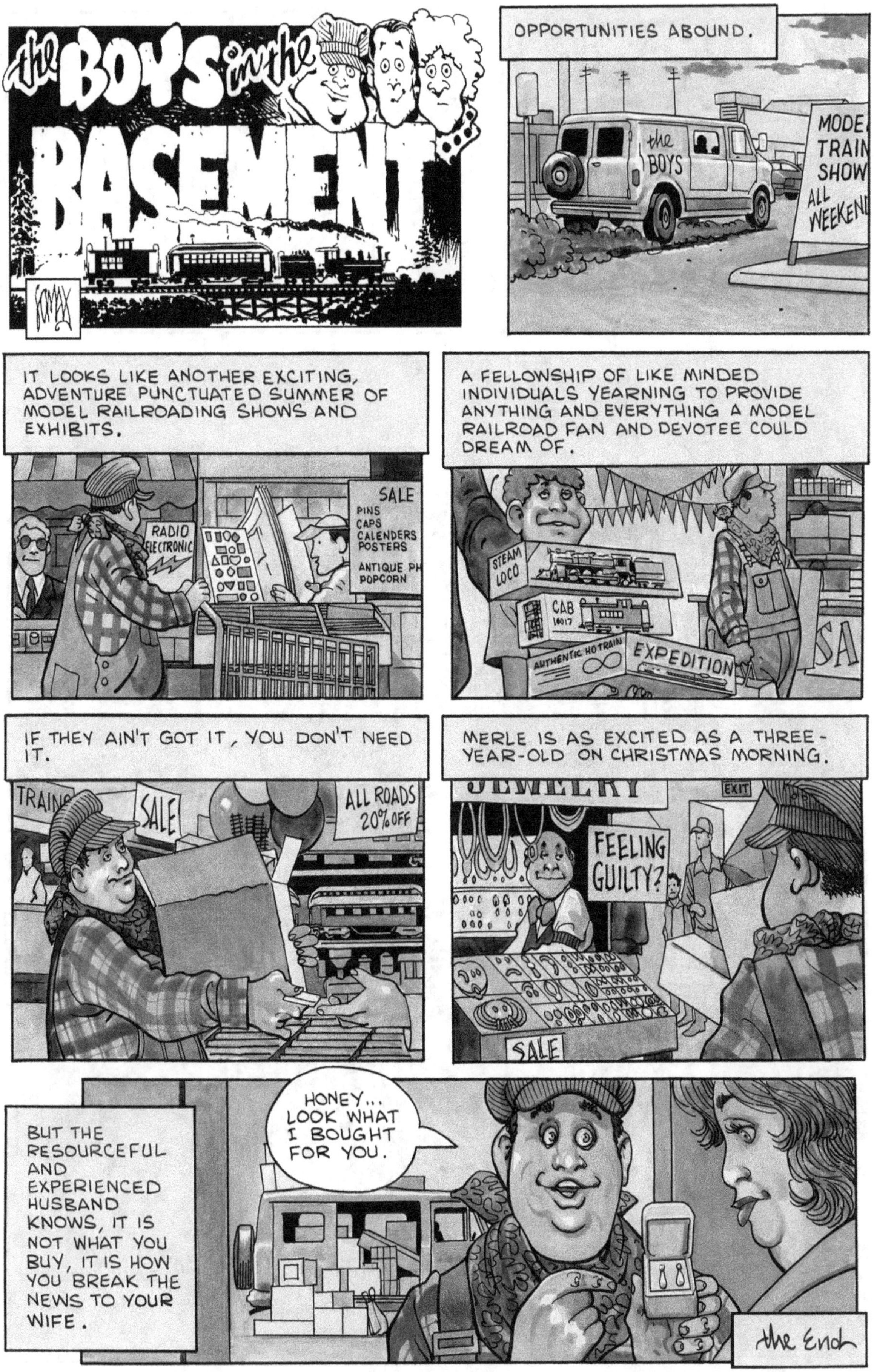
the BOYS in the BASEMENT
OPPORTUNITIES ABOUND.
the BOYS
MODE TRAIN SHOW ALL WEEKEN
IT LOOKS LIKE ANOTHER EXCITING, ADVENTURE PUNCTUATED SUMMER OF MODEL RAILROADING SHOWS AND EXHIBITS.
RADIO ELECTRONIC
SALE PINS CAPS CALENDERS POSTERS ANTIQUE PH POPCORN
A FELLOWSHIP OF LIKE MINDED INDIVIDUALS YEARNING TO PROVIDE ANYTHING AND EVERYTHING A MODEL RAILROAD FAN AND DEVOTEE COULD DREAM OF.
STEAM LOCO
CAB 10017
AUTHENTIC HO TRAIN
EXPEDITION
IF THEY AIN'T GOT IT, YOU DON'T NEED IT.
TRAIN
SALE
ALL ROADS 20% OFF
MERLE IS AS EXCITED AS A THREE-YEAR-OLD ON CHRISTMAS MORNING.
JEWELRY
EXIT
FEELING GUILTY?
SALE
BUT THE RESOURCEFUL AND EXPERIENCED HUSBAND KNOWS, IT IS NOT WHAT YOU BUY, IT IS HOW YOU BREAK THE NEWS TO YOUR WIFE.
HONEY... LOOK WHAT I BOUGHT FOR YOU.
the End

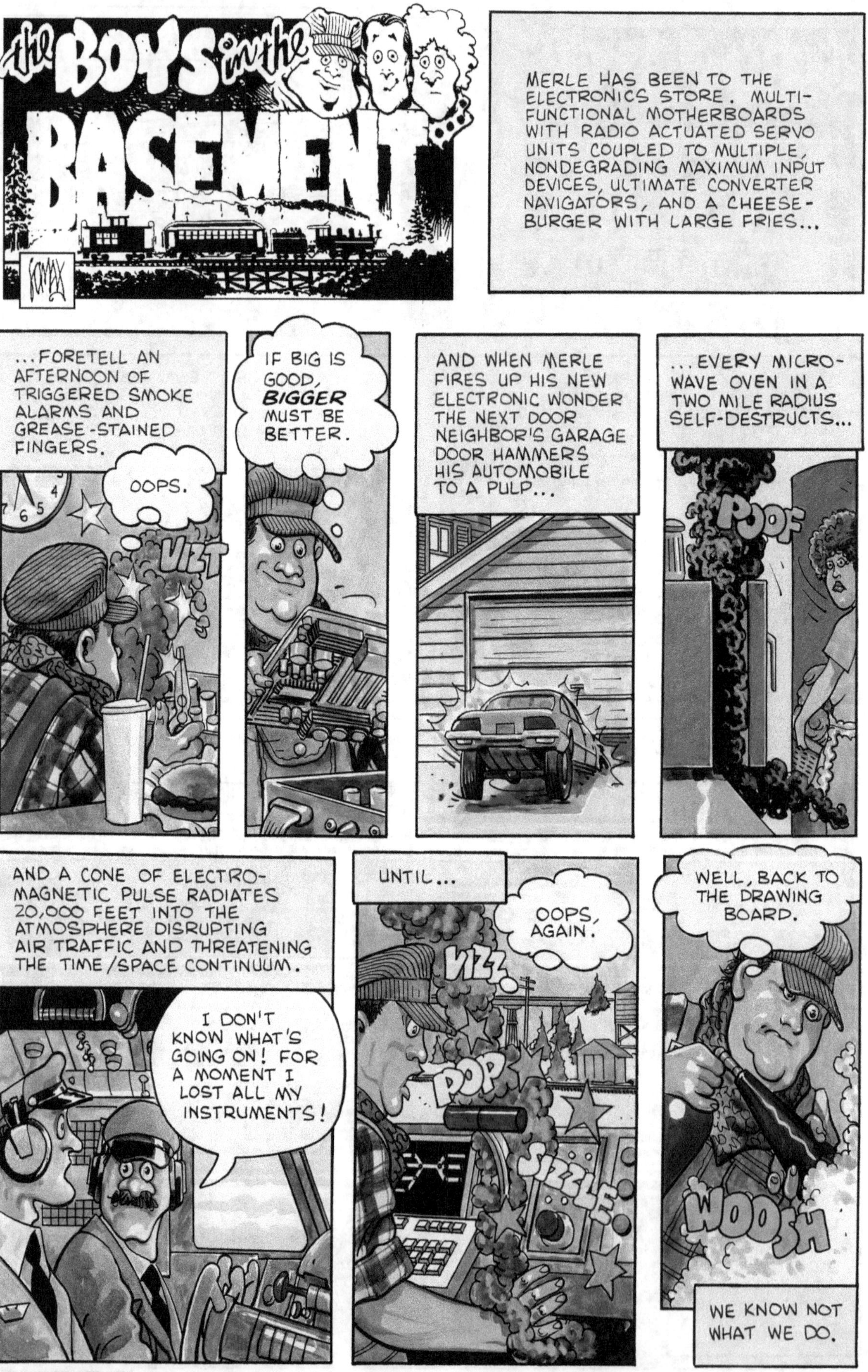
the BOYS in the BASEMENT
MERLE HAS BEEN TO THE ELECTRONICS STORE. MULTI-FUNCTIONAL MOTHERBOARDS WITH RADIO ACTUATED SERVO UNITS COUPLED TO MULTIPLE, NONDEGRADING MAXIMUM INPUT DEVICES, ULTIMATE CONVERTER NAVIGATORS, AND A CHEESE-BURGER WITH LARGE FRIES...
...FORETELL AN AFTERNOON OF TRIGGERED SMOKE ALARMS AND GREASE-STAINED FINGERS.
OOPS.
VIZT
IF BIG IS GOOD, **BIGGER** MUST BE BETTER.
AND WHEN MERLE FIRES UP HIS NEW ELECTRONIC WONDER THE NEXT DOOR NEIGHBOR'S GARAGE DOOR HAMMERS HIS AUTOMOBILE TO A PULP...
...EVERY MICRO-WAVE OVEN IN A TWO MILE RADIUS SELF-DESTRUCTS...
POOF
AND A CONE OF ELECTRO-MAGNETIC PULSE RADIATES 20,000 FEET INTO THE ATMOSPHERE DISRUPTING AIR TRAFFIC AND THREATENING THE TIME/SPACE CONTINUUM.
I DON'T KNOW WHAT'S GOING ON! FOR A MOMENT I LOST ALL MY INSTRUMENTS!
UNTIL...
OOPS, AGAIN.
VIZZ
POP
SIZZLE
WELL, BACK TO THE DRAWING BOARD.
WOOSH
WE KNOW NOT WHAT WE DO.

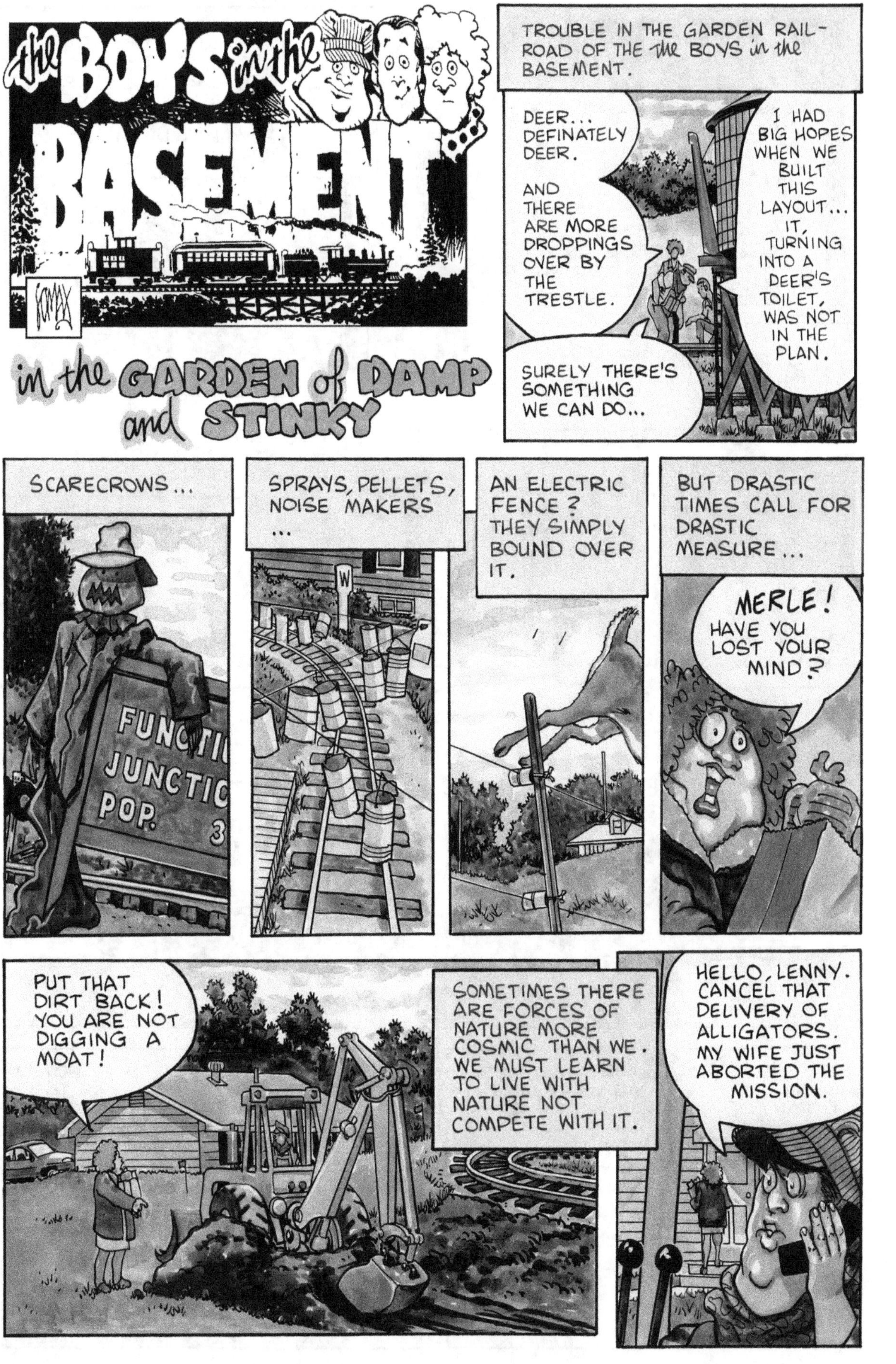
the BOYS in the BASEMENT
in the GARDEN of DAMP and STINKY
TROUBLE IN THE GARDEN RAILROAD OF THE the BOYS in the BASEMENT.
DEER... DEFINATELY DEER.
AND THERE ARE MORE DROPPINGS OVER BY THE TRESTLE.
I HAD BIG HOPES WHEN WE BUILT THIS LAYOUT... IT, TURNING INTO A DEER'S TOILET, WAS NOT IN THE PLAN.
SURELY THERE'S SOMETHING WE CAN DO...
SCARECROWS...
SPRAYS, PELLETS, NOISE MAKERS ...
W
AN ELECTRIC FENCE? THEY SIMPLY BOUND OVER IT.
BUT DRASTIC TIMES CALL FOR DRASTIC MEASURE...
MERLE! HAVE YOU LOST YOUR MIND?
PUT THAT DIRT BACK! YOU ARE NOT DIGGING A MOAT!
SOMETIMES THERE ARE FORCES OF NATURE MORE COSMIC THAN WE. WE MUST LEARN TO LIVE WITH NATURE NOT COMPETE WITH IT.
HELLO, LENNY. CANCEL THAT DELIVERY OF ALLIGATORS. MY WIFE JUST ABORTED THE MISSION.

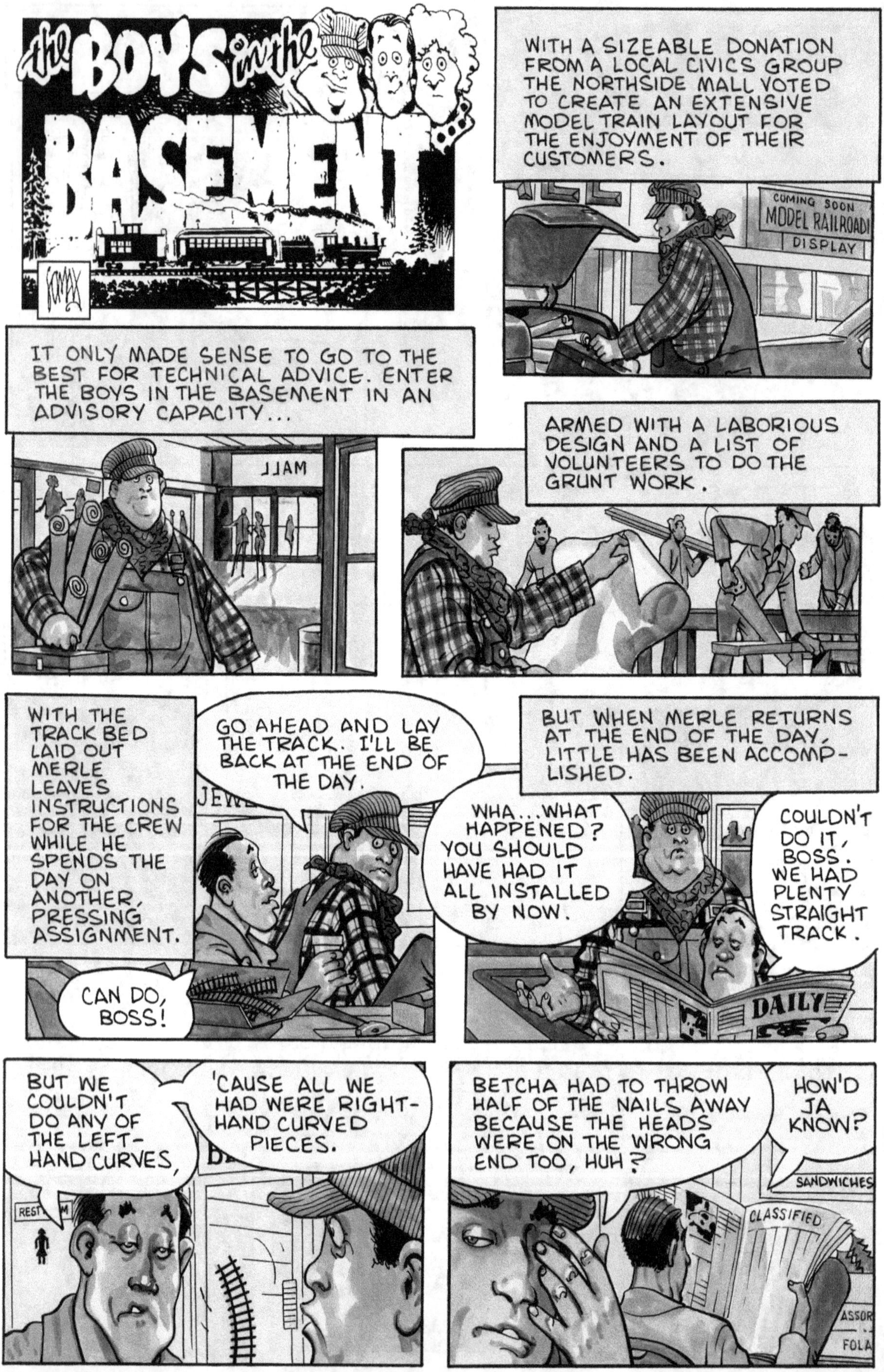
the BOYS in the BASEMENT
WITH A SIZEABLE DONATION FROM A LOCAL CIVICS GROUP THE NORTHSIDE MALL VOTED TO CREATE AN EXTENSIVE MODEL TRAIN LAYOUT FOR THE ENJOYMENT OF THEIR CUSTOMERS.
COMING SOON MODEL RAILROADI DISPLAY
IT ONLY MADE SENSE TO GO TO THE BEST FOR TECHNICAL ADVICE. ENTER THE BOYS IN THE BASEMENT IN AN ADVISORY CAPACITY...
MALL
ARMED WITH A LABORIOUS DESIGN AND A LIST OF VOLUNTEERS TO DO THE GRUNT WORK.
WITH THE TRACK BED LAID OUT MERLE LEAVES INSTRUCTIONS FOR THE CREW WHILE HE SPENDS THE DAY ON ANOTHER, PRESSING ASSIGNMENT.
GO AHEAD AND LAY THE TRACK. I'LL BE BACK AT THE END OF THE DAY.
CAN DO, BOSS!
BUT WHEN MERLE RETURNS AT THE END OF THE DAY, LITTLE HAS BEEN ACCOMP-LISHED.
WHA...WHAT HAPPENED? YOU SHOULD HAVE HAD IT ALL INSTALLED BY NOW.
COULDN'T DO IT, BOSS. WE HAD PLENTY STRAIGHT TRACK.
DAILY
BUT WE COULDN'T DO ANY OF THE LEFT-HAND CURVES,
'CAUSE ALL WE HAD WERE RIGHT-HAND CURVED PIECES.
BETCHA HAD TO THROW HALF OF THE NAILS AWAY BECAUSE THE HEADS WERE ON THE WRONG END TOO, HUH?
HOW'D JA KNOW?
SANDWICHES
CLASSIFIED

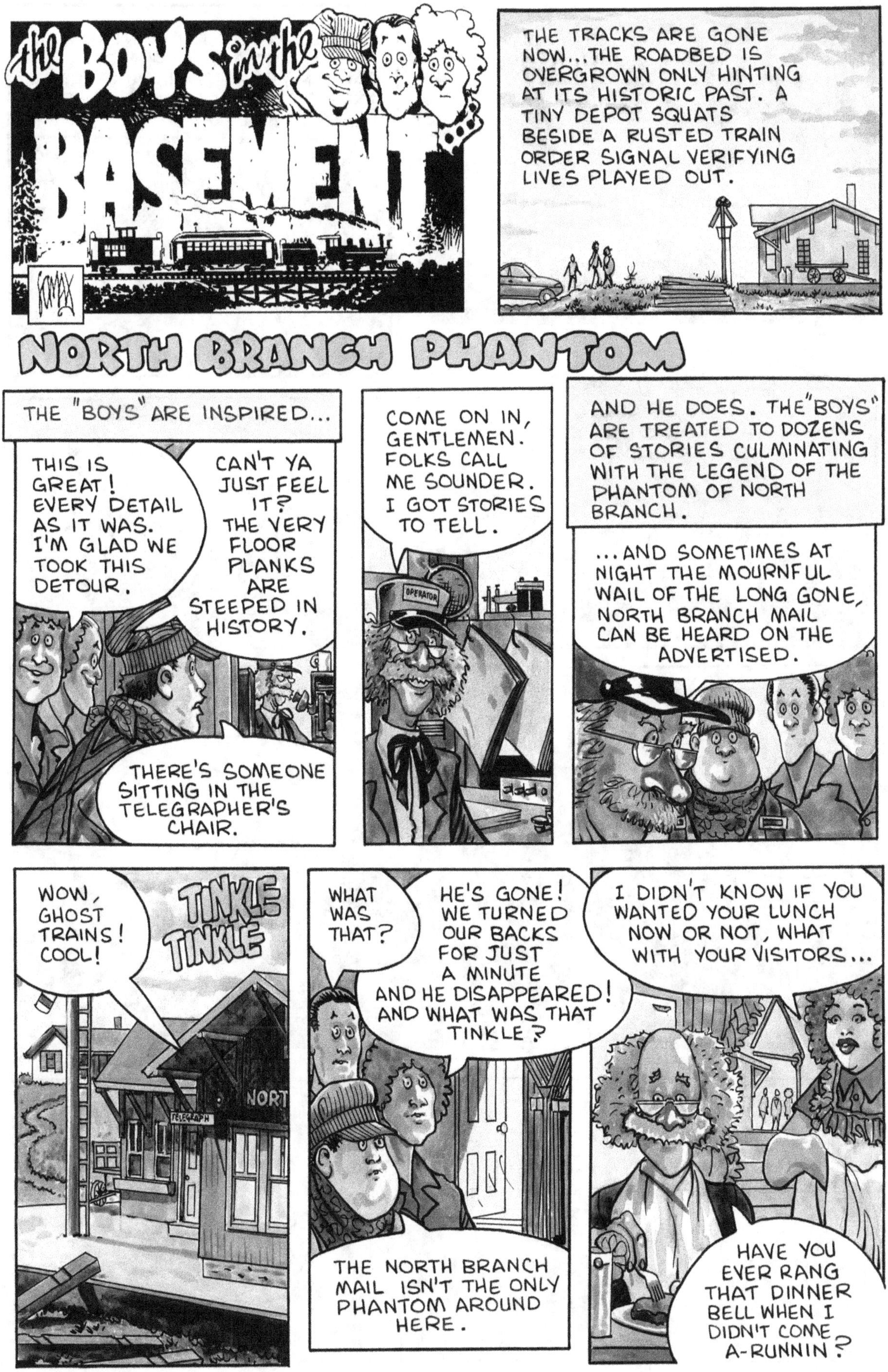
the BOYS in the BASEMENT
THE TRACKS ARE GONE NOW...THE ROADBED IS OVERGROWN ONLY HINTING AT ITS HISTORIC PAST. A TINY DEPOT SQUATS BESIDE A RUSTED TRAIN ORDER SIGNAL VERIFYING LIVES PLAYED OUT.
NORTH BRANCH PHANTOM
THE "BOYS" ARE INSPIRED...
THIS IS GREAT! EVERY DETAIL AS IT WAS. I'M GLAD WE TOOK THIS DETOUR.
CAN'T YA JUST FEEL IT? THE VERY FLOOR PLANKS ARE STEEPED IN HISTORY.
THERE'S SOMEONE SITTING IN THE TELEGRAPHER'S CHAIR.
COME ON IN, GENTLEMEN. FOLKS CALL ME SOUNDER. I GOT STORIES TO TELL.
OPERATOR
AND HE DOES. THE "BOYS" ARE TREATED TO DOZENS OF STORIES CULMINATING WITH THE LEGEND OF THE PHANTOM OF NORTH BRANCH.
...AND SOMETIMES AT NIGHT THE MOURNFUL WAIL OF THE LONG GONE, NORTH BRANCH MAIL CAN BE HEARD ON THE ADVERTISED.
WOW, GHOST TRAINS! COOL!
TINKLE TINKLE
TELEGRAPH
NORT
WHAT WAS THAT?
HE'S GONE! WE TURNED OUR BACKS FOR JUST A MINUTE AND HE DISAPPEARED! AND WHAT WAS THAT TINKLE?
THE NORTH BRANCH MAIL ISN'T THE ONLY PHANTOM AROUND HERE.
I DIDN'T KNOW IF YOU WANTED YOUR LUNCH NOW OR NOT, WHAT WITH YOUR VISITORS...
HAVE YOU EVER RANG THAT DINNER BELL WHEN I DIDN'T COME A-RUNNIN?

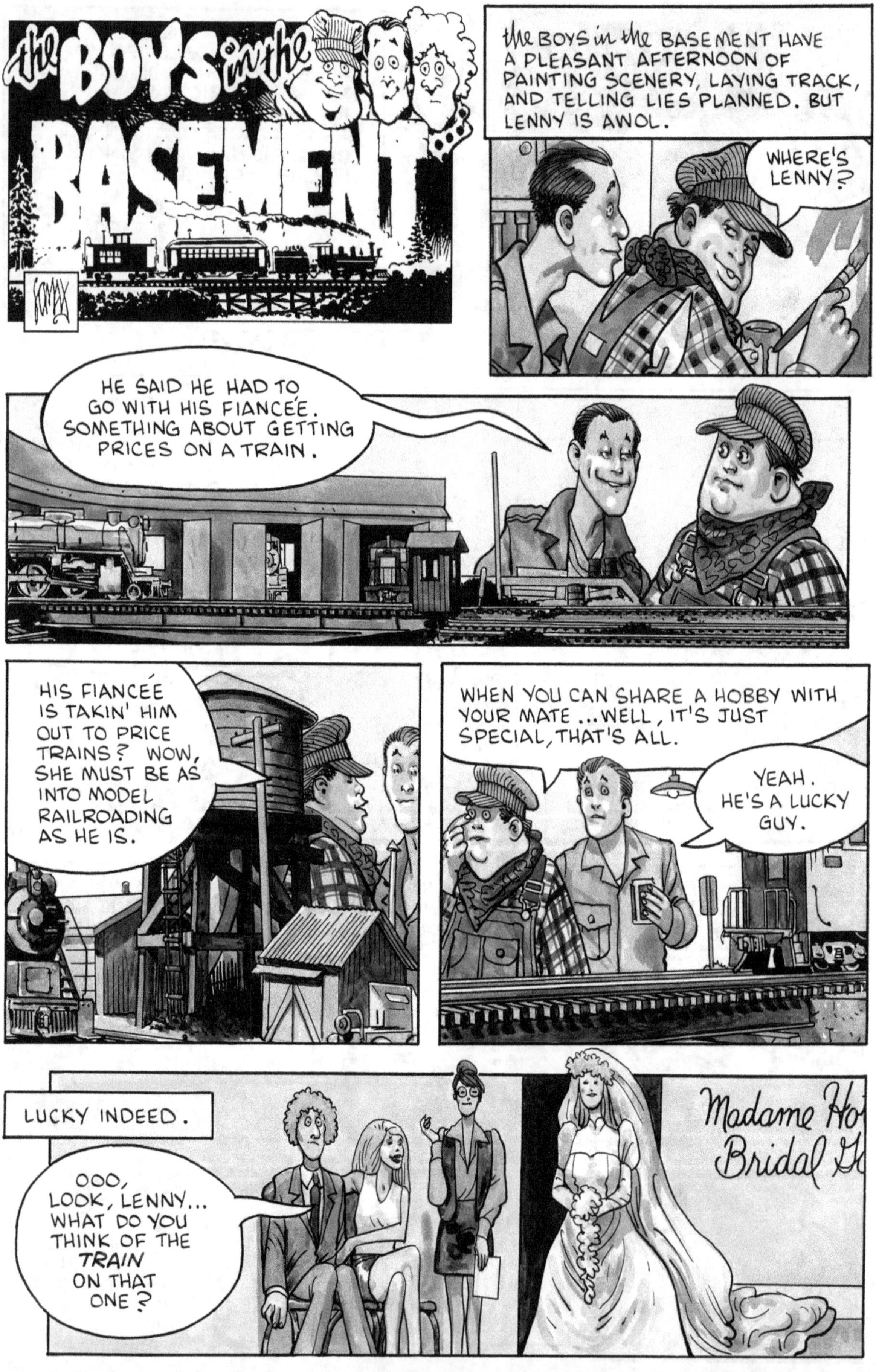
the BOYS in the BASEMENT
the BOYS in the BASEMENT HAVE A PLEASANT AFTERNOON OF PAINTING SCENERY, LAYING TRACK, AND TELLING LIES PLANNED. BUT LENNY IS AWOL.
WHERE'S LENNY?
HE SAID HE HAD TO GO WITH HIS FIANCÉE. SOMETHING ABOUT GETTING PRICES ON A TRAIN.
HIS FIANCÉE IS TAKIN' HIM OUT TO PRICE TRAINS? WOW, SHE MUST BE AS INTO MODEL RAILROADING AS HE IS.
WHEN YOU CAN SHARE A HOBBY WITH YOUR MATE ... WELL, IT'S JUST SPECIAL, THAT'S ALL.
YEAH. HE'S A LUCKY GUY.
LUCKY INDEED.
OOO, LOOK, LENNY... WHAT DO YOU THINK OF THE *TRAIN* ON THAT ONE?

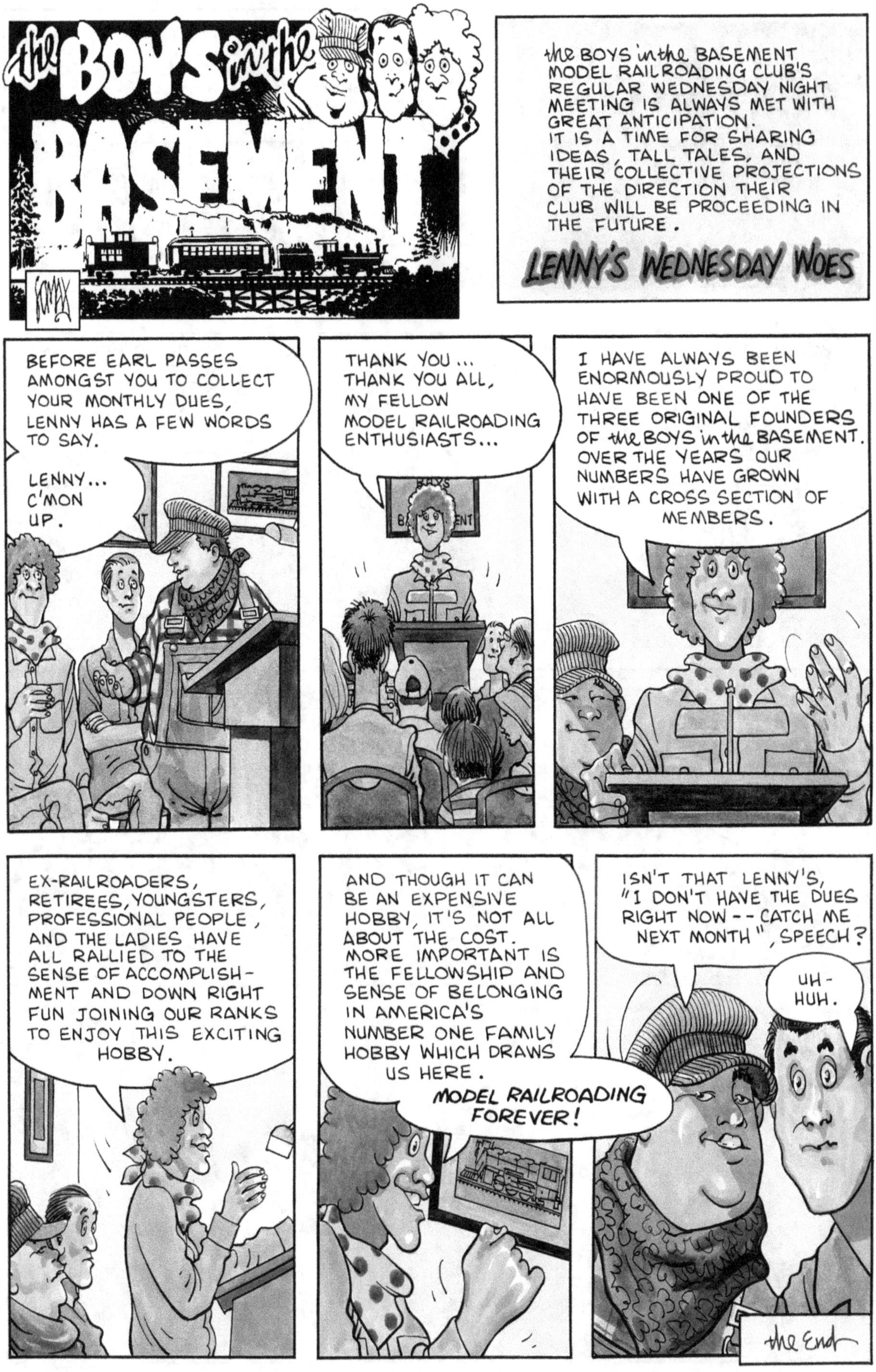
the BOYS in the BASEMENT
the BOYS in the BASEMENT MODEL RAILROADING CLUB'S REGULAR WEDNESDAY NIGHT MEETING IS ALWAYS MET WITH GREAT ANTICIPATION. IT IS A TIME FOR SHARING IDEAS, TALL TALES, AND THEIR COLLECTIVE PROJECTIONS OF THE DIRECTION THEIR CLUB WILL BE PROCEEDING IN THE FUTURE.
LENNY'S WEDNESDAY WOES
BEFORE EARL PASSES AMONGST YOU TO COLLECT YOUR MONTHLY DUES, LENNY HAS A FEW WORDS TO SAY.
LENNY... C'MON UP.
THANK YOU... THANK YOU ALL, MY FELLOW MODEL RAILROADING ENTHUSIASTS...
I HAVE ALWAYS BEEN ENORMOUSLY PROUD TO HAVE BEEN ONE OF THE THREE ORIGINAL FOUNDERS OF the BOYS in the BASEMENT. OVER THE YEARS OUR NUMBERS HAVE GROWN WITH A CROSS SECTION OF MEMBERS.
EX-RAILROADERS, RETIREES, YOUNGSTERS, PROFESSIONAL PEOPLE, AND THE LADIES HAVE ALL RALLIED TO THE SENSE OF ACCOMPLISH-MENT AND DOWN RIGHT FUN JOINING OUR RANKS TO ENJOY THIS EXCITING HOBBY.
AND THOUGH IT CAN BE AN EXPENSIVE HOBBY, IT'S NOT ALL ABOUT THE COST. MORE IMPORTANT IS THE FELLOWSHIP AND SENSE OF BELONGING IN AMERICA'S NUMBER ONE FAMILY HOBBY WHICH DRAWS US HERE.
MODEL RAILROADING FOREVER!
ISN'T THAT LENNY'S, "I DON'T HAVE THE DUES RIGHT NOW -- CATCH ME NEXT MONTH", SPEECH?
UH-HUH.
the End

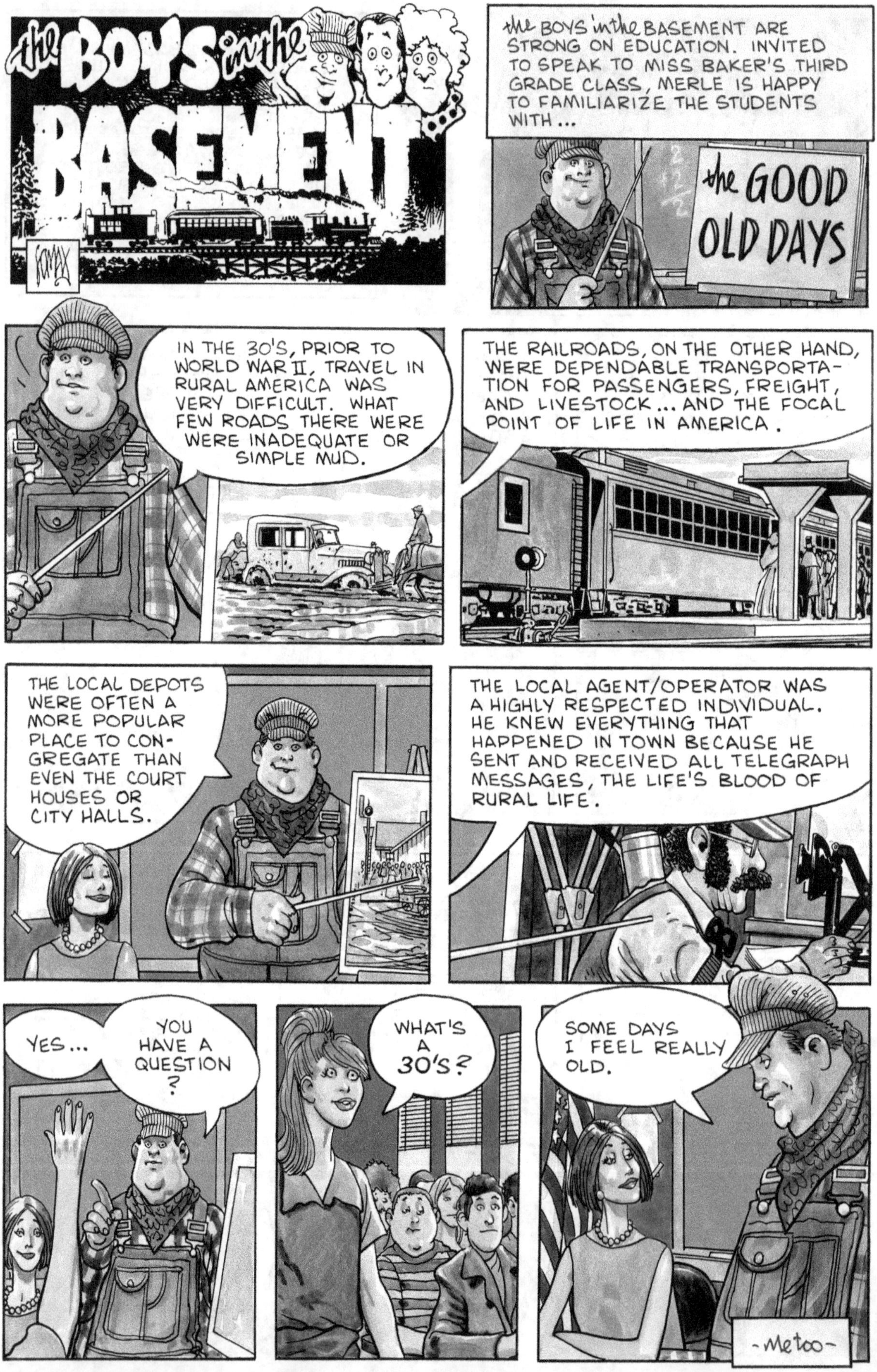
the BOYS in the BASEMENT
SOMAX
the BOYS in the BASEMENT ARE STRONG ON EDUCATION. INVITED TO SPEAK TO MISS BAKER'S THIRD GRADE CLASS, MERLE IS HAPPY TO FAMILIARIZE THE STUDENTS WITH...
the GOOD OLD DAYS
IN THE 30'S, PRIOR TO WORLD WAR II, TRAVEL IN RURAL AMERICA WAS VERY DIFFICULT. WHAT FEW ROADS THERE WERE WERE INADEQUATE OR SIMPLE MUD.
THE RAILROADS, ON THE OTHER HAND, WERE DEPENDABLE TRANSPORTA-TION FOR PASSENGERS, FREIGHT, AND LIVESTOCK... AND THE FOCAL POINT OF LIFE IN AMERICA.
THE LOCAL DEPOTS WERE OFTEN A MORE POPULAR PLACE TO CON-GREGATE THAN EVEN THE COURT HOUSES OR CITY HALLS.
THE LOCAL AGENT/OPERATOR WAS A HIGHLY RESPECTED INDIVIDUAL. HE KNEW EVERYTHING THAT HAPPENED IN TOWN BECAUSE HE SENT AND RECEIVED ALL TELEGRAPH MESSAGES, THE LIFE'S BLOOD OF RURAL LIFE.
YES...
YOU HAVE A QUESTION ?
WHAT'S A 30'S?
SOME DAYS I FEEL REALLY OLD.
-Me too-

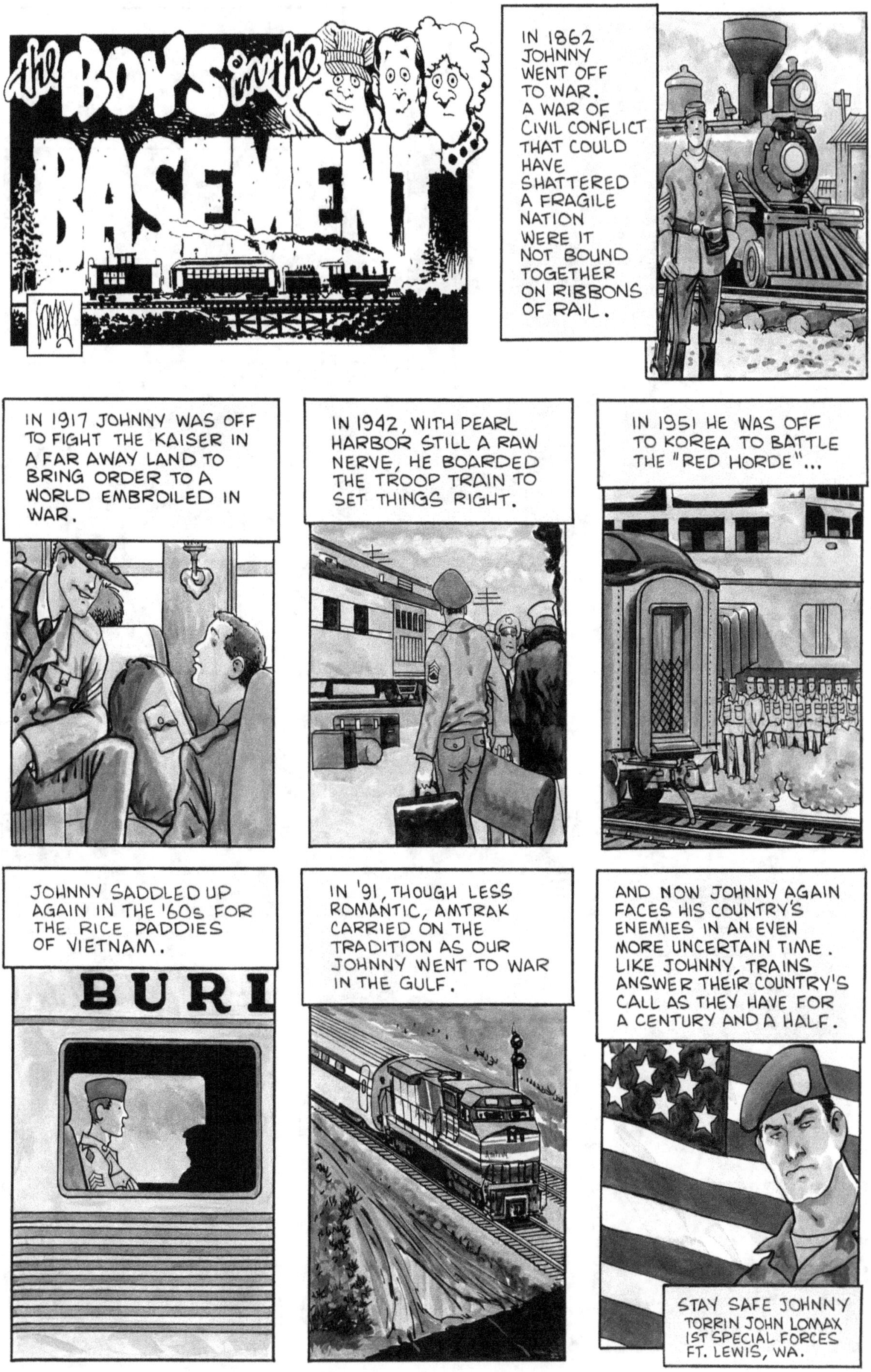
the BOYS in the BASEMENT
IN 1862 JOHNNY WENT OFF TO WAR. A WAR OF CIVIL CONFLICT THAT COULD HAVE SHATTERED A FRAGILE NATION WERE IT NOT BOUND TOGETHER ON RIBBONS OF RAIL.
IN 1917 JOHNNY WAS OFF TO FIGHT THE KAISER IN A FAR AWAY LAND TO BRING ORDER TO A WORLD EMBROILED IN WAR.
IN 1942, WITH PEARL HARBOR STILL A RAW NERVE, HE BOARDED THE TROOP TRAIN TO SET THINGS RIGHT.
IN 1951 HE WAS OFF TO KOREA TO BATTLE THE "RED HORDE"...
JOHNNY SADDLED UP AGAIN IN THE '60s FOR THE RICE PADDIES OF VIETNAM.
BURL
IN '91, THOUGH LESS ROMANTIC, AMTRAK CARRIED ON THE TRADITION AS OUR JOHNNY WENT TO WAR IN THE GULF.
AND NOW JOHNNY AGAIN FACES HIS COUNTRY'S ENEMIES IN AN EVEN MORE UNCERTAIN TIME. LIKE JOHNNY, TRAINS ANSWER THEIR COUNTRY'S CALL AS THEY HAVE FOR A CENTURY AND A HALF.
STAY SAFE JOHNNY
TORRIN JOHN LOMAX
1ST SPECIAL FORCES
FT. LEWIS, WA.

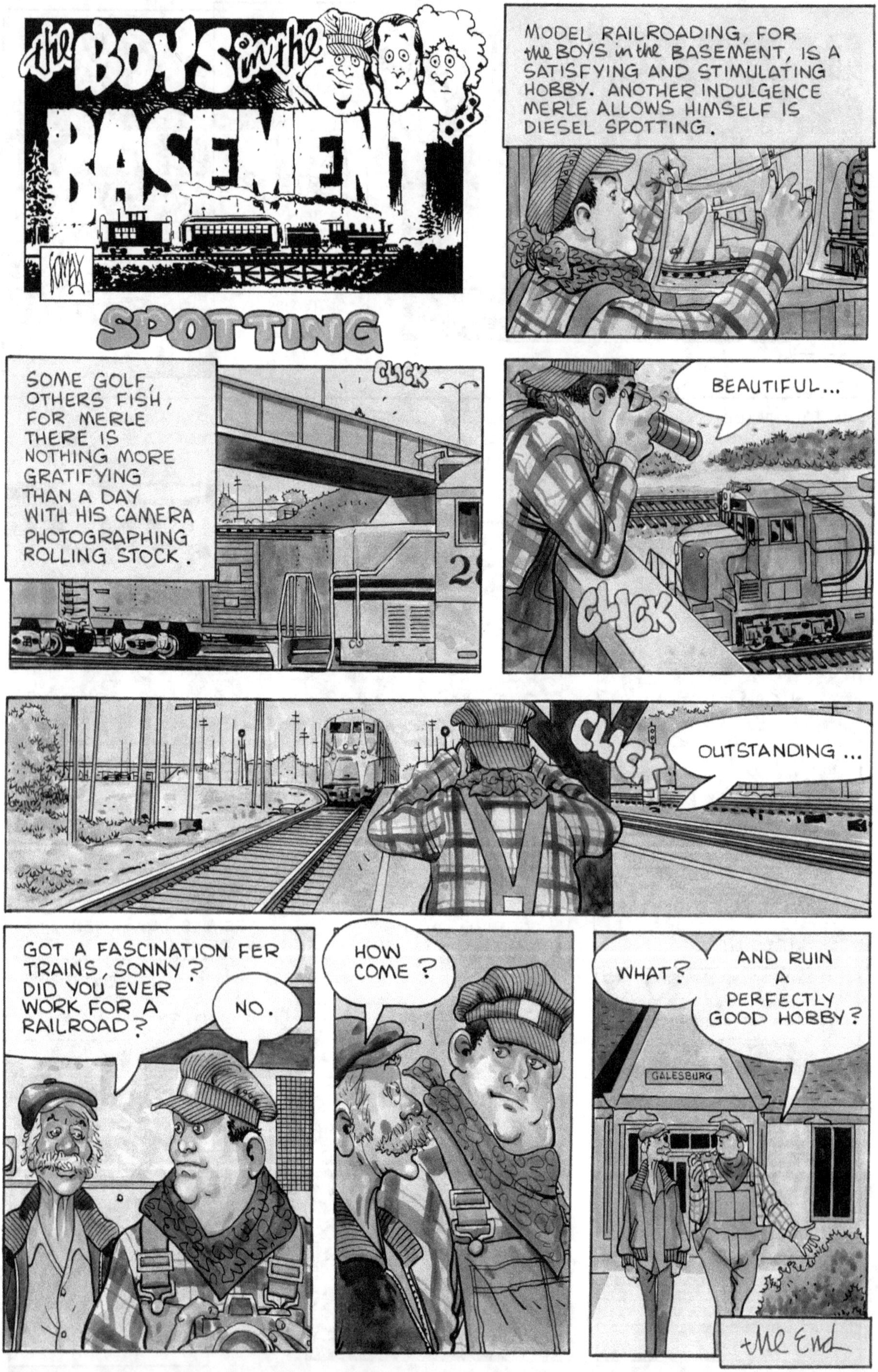
the BOYS in the BASEMENT
SPOTTING
MODEL RAILROADING, FOR the BOYS in the BASEMENT, IS A SATISFYING AND STIMULATING HOBBY. ANOTHER INDULGENCE MERLE ALLOWS HIMSELF IS DIESEL SPOTTING.
SOME GOLF, OTHERS FISH, FOR MERLE THERE IS NOTHING MORE GRATIFYING THAN A DAY WITH HIS CAMERA PHOTOGRAPHING ROLLING STOCK.
CLICK
BEAUTIFUL...
CLICK
CLICK
OUTSTANDING ...
GOT A FASCINATION FER TRAINS, SONNY? DID YOU EVER WORK FOR A RAILROAD?
NO.
HOW COME?
WHAT?
AND RUIN A PERFECTLY GOOD HOBBY?
GALESBURG
the End

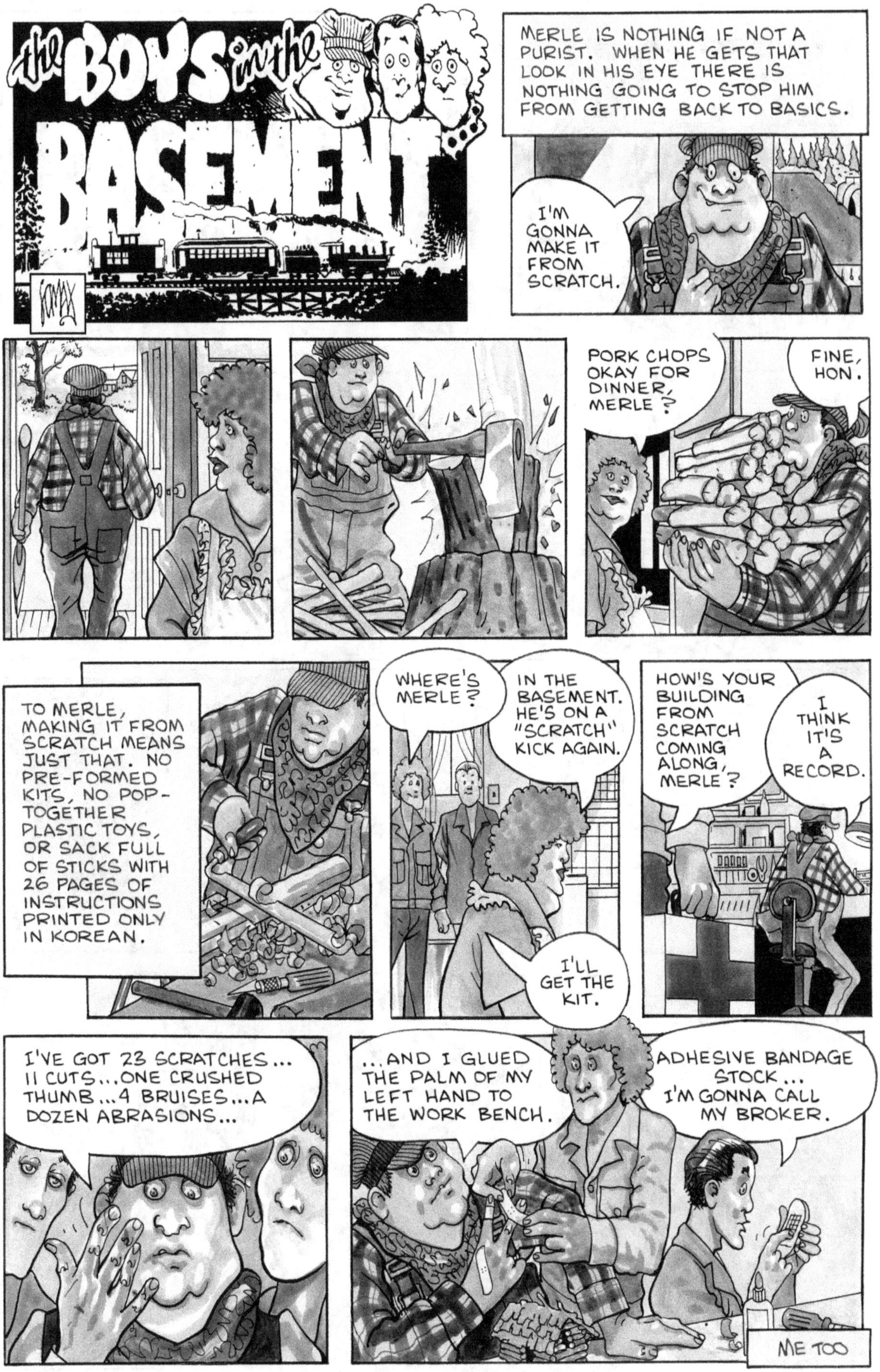
the BOYS in the BASEMENT
SOMAX
MERLE IS NOTHING IF NOT A PURIST. WHEN HE GETS THAT LOOK IN HIS EYE THERE IS NOTHING GOING TO STOP HIM FROM GETTING BACK TO BASICS.
I'M GONNA MAKE IT FROM SCRATCH.
PORK CHOPS OKAY FOR DINNER, MERLE?
FINE, HON.
TO MERLE, MAKING IT FROM SCRATCH MEANS JUST THAT. NO PRE-FORMED KITS, NO POP-TOGETHER PLASTIC TOYS, OR SACK FULL OF STICKS WITH 26 PAGES OF INSTRUCTIONS PRINTED ONLY IN KOREAN.
WHERE'S MERLE?
IN THE BASEMENT. HE'S ON A "SCRATCH" KICK AGAIN.
I'LL GET THE KIT.
HOW'S YOUR BUILDING FROM SCRATCH COMING ALONG, MERLE?
I THINK IT'S A RECORD.
I'VE GOT 23 SCRATCHES... 11 CUTS...ONE CRUSHED THUMB...4 BRUISES...A DOZEN ABRASIONS...
...AND I GLUED THE PALM OF MY LEFT HAND TO THE WORK BENCH.
ADHESIVE BANDAGE STOCK... I'M GONNA CALL MY BROKER.
ME TOO

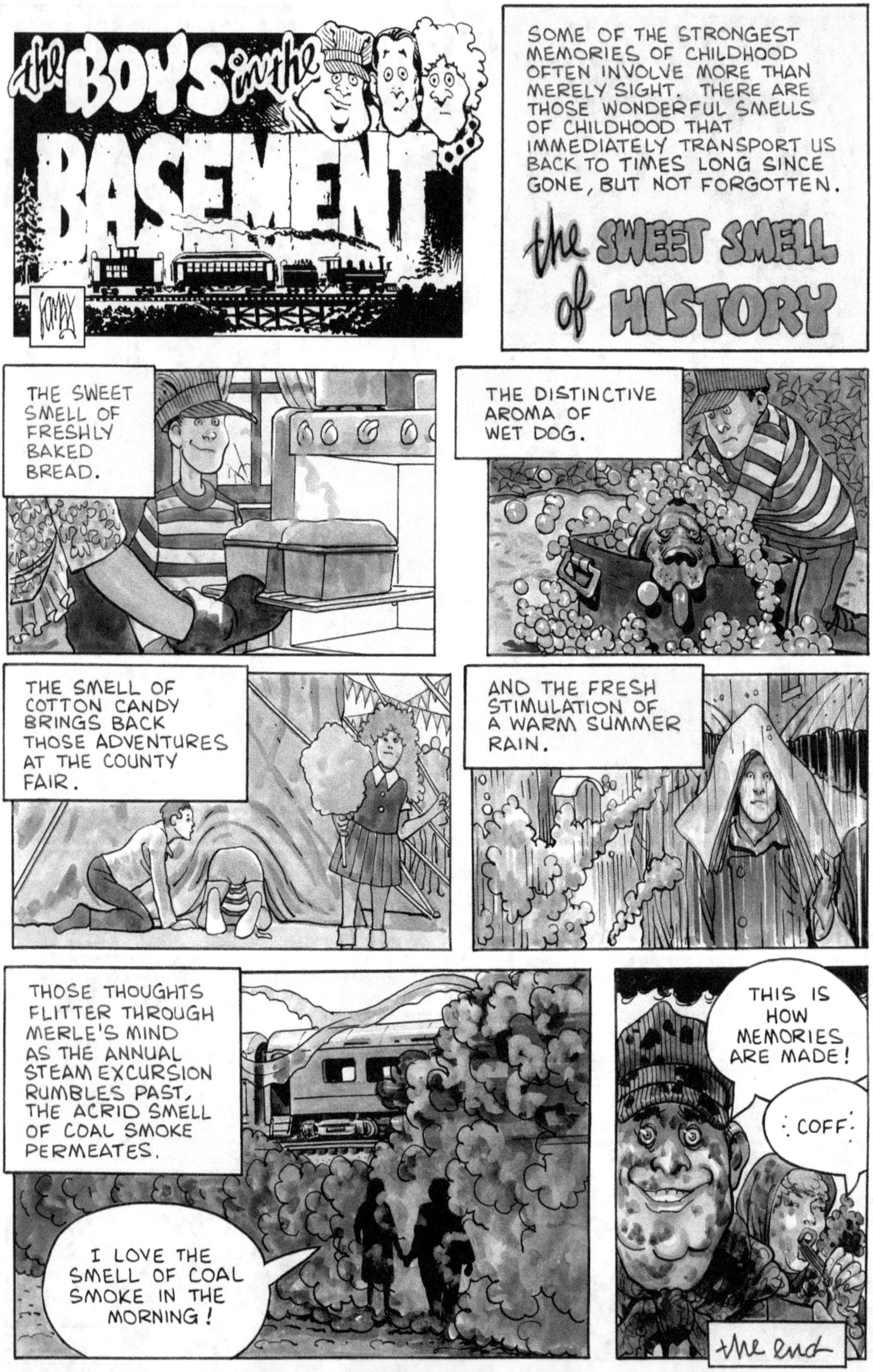
the BOYS in the BASEMENT
SOME OF THE STRONGEST MEMORIES OF CHILDHOOD OFTEN INVOLVE MORE THAN MERELY SIGHT. THERE ARE THOSE WONDERFUL SMELLS OF CHILDHOOD THAT IMMEDIATELY TRANSPORT US BACK TO TIMES LONG SINCE GONE, BUT NOT FORGOTTEN.
the SWEET SMELL of HISTORY
THE SWEET SMELL OF FRESHLY BAKED BREAD.
THE DISTINCTIVE AROMA OF WET DOG.
THE SMELL OF COTTON CANDY BRINGS BACK THOSE ADVENTURES AT THE COUNTY FAIR.
AND THE FRESH STIMULATION OF A WARM SUMMER RAIN.
THOSE THOUGHTS FLITTER THROUGH MERLE'S MIND AS THE ANNUAL STEAM EXCURSION RUMBLES PAST, THE ACRID SMELL OF COAL SMOKE PERMEATES.
I LOVE THE SMELL OF COAL SMOKE IN THE MORNING!
THIS IS HOW MEMORIES ARE MADE!
COFF
the end

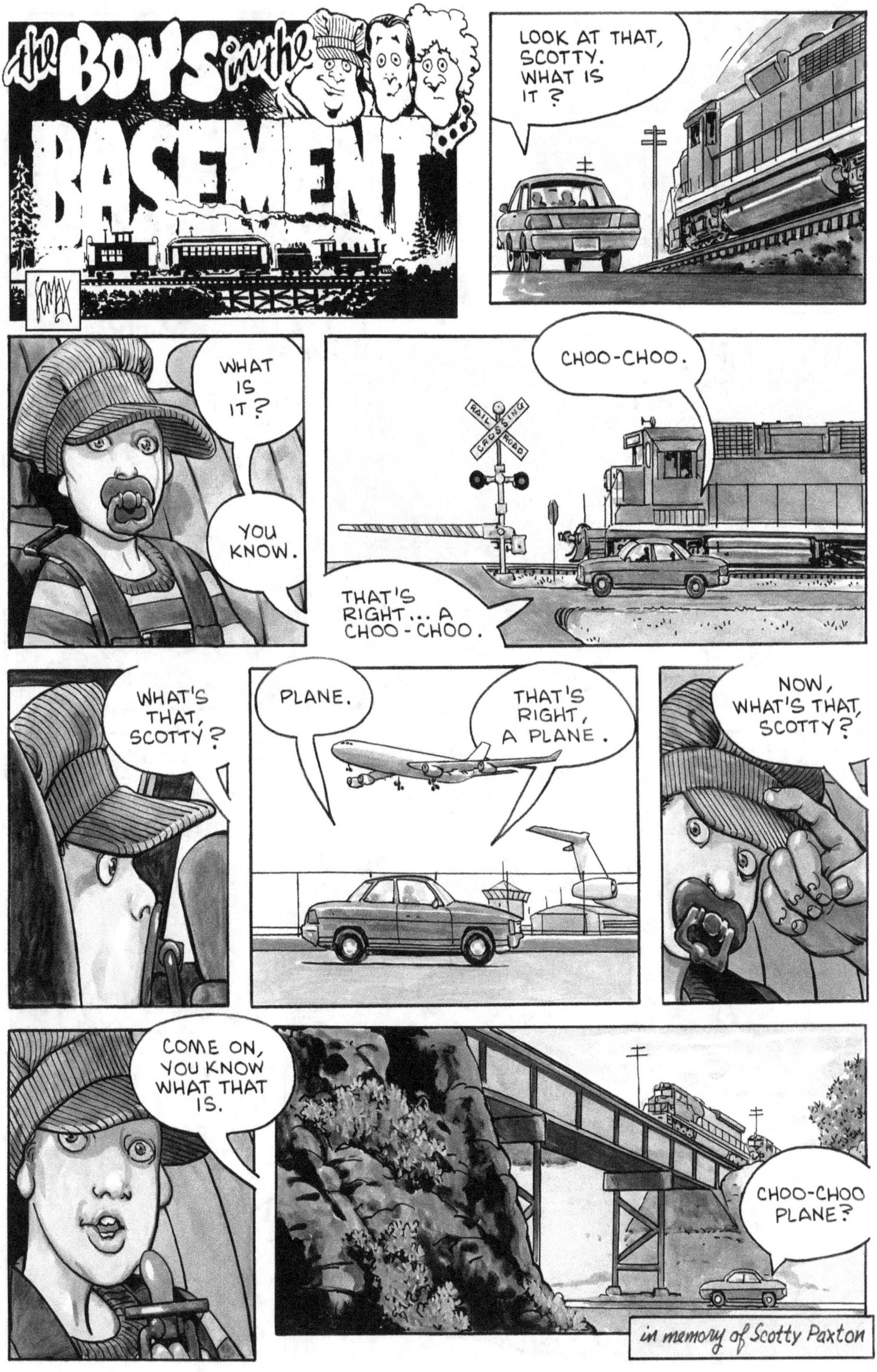
the BOYS in the BASEMENT
LOOK AT THAT, SCOTTY. WHAT IS IT ?
WHAT IS IT?
YOU KNOW.
CHOO-CHOO.
RAIL ROAD CROSSING
THAT'S RIGHT... A CHOO-CHOO.
WHAT'S THAT, SCOTTY?
PLANE.
THAT'S RIGHT, A PLANE.
NOW, WHAT'S THAT, SCOTTY?
COME ON, YOU KNOW WHAT THAT IS.
CHOO-CHOO PLANE?
in memory of Scotty Paxton

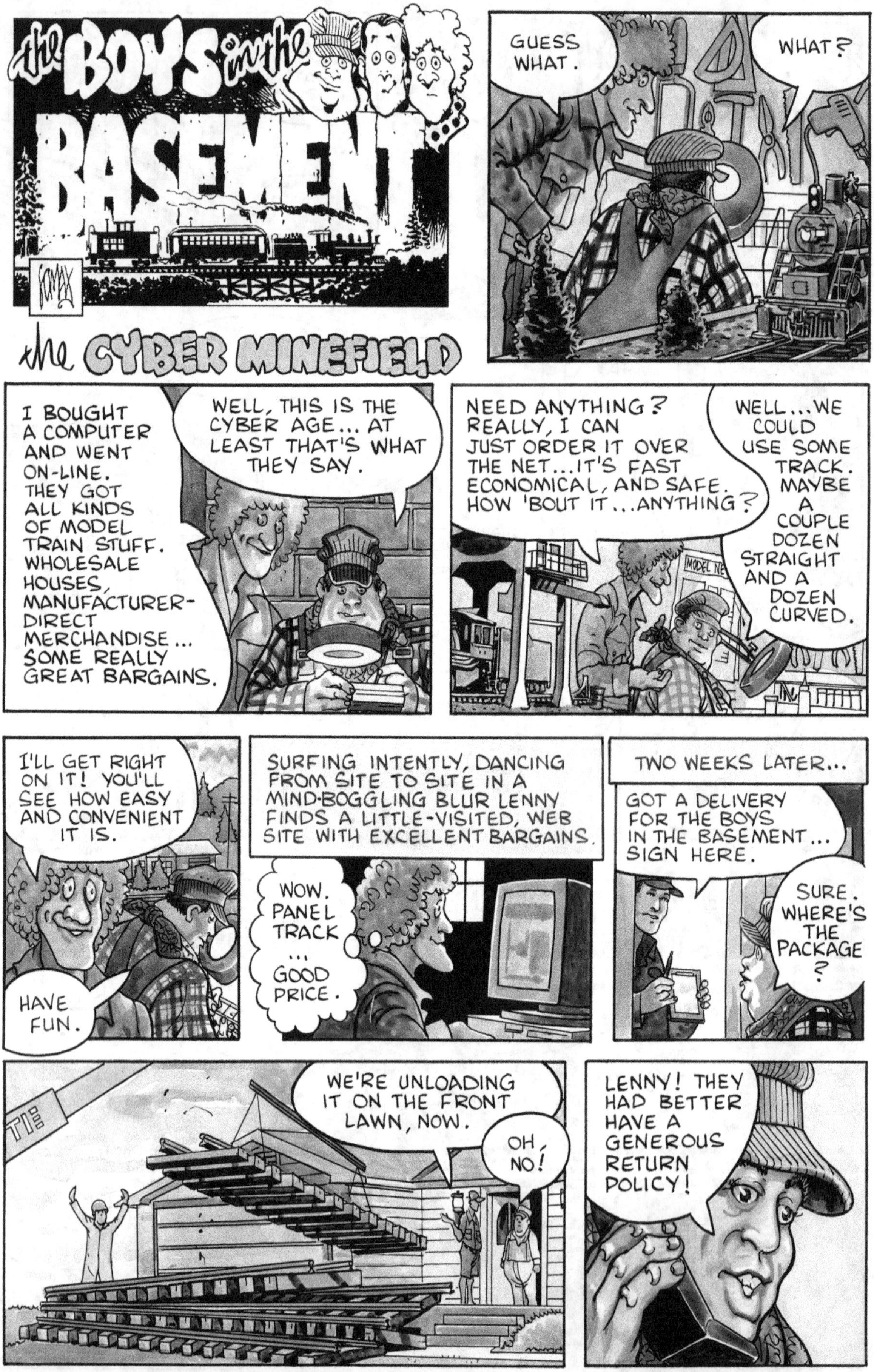
the BOYS in the BASEMENT
the CYBER MINEFIELD
GUESS WHAT.
WHAT?
I BOUGHT A COMPUTER AND WENT ON-LINE. THEY GOT ALL KINDS OF MODEL TRAIN STUFF. WHOLESALE HOUSES, MANUFACTURER-DIRECT MERCHANDISE... SOME REALLY GREAT BARGAINS.
WELL, THIS IS THE CYBER AGE... AT LEAST THAT'S WHAT THEY SAY.
NEED ANYTHING? REALLY, I CAN JUST ORDER IT OVER THE NET... IT'S FAST ECONOMICAL, AND SAFE. HOW 'BOUT IT... ANYTHING?
WELL... WE COULD USE SOME TRACK. MAYBE A COUPLE DOZEN STRAIGHT AND A DOZEN CURVED.
I'LL GET RIGHT ON IT! YOU'LL SEE HOW EASY AND CONVENIENT IT IS.
HAVE FUN.
SURFING INTENTLY, DANCING FROM SITE TO SITE IN A MIND-BOGGLING BLUR LENNY FINDS A LITTLE-VISITED, WEB SITE WITH EXCELLENT BARGAINS.
WOW. PANEL TRACK ... GOOD PRICE.
TWO WEEKS LATER...
GOT A DELIVERY FOR THE BOYS IN THE BASEMENT... SIGN HERE.
SURE. WHERE'S THE PACKAGE?
WE'RE UNLOADING IT ON THE FRONT LAWN, NOW.
OH, NO!
LENNY! THEY HAD BETTER HAVE A GENEROUS RETURN POLICY!

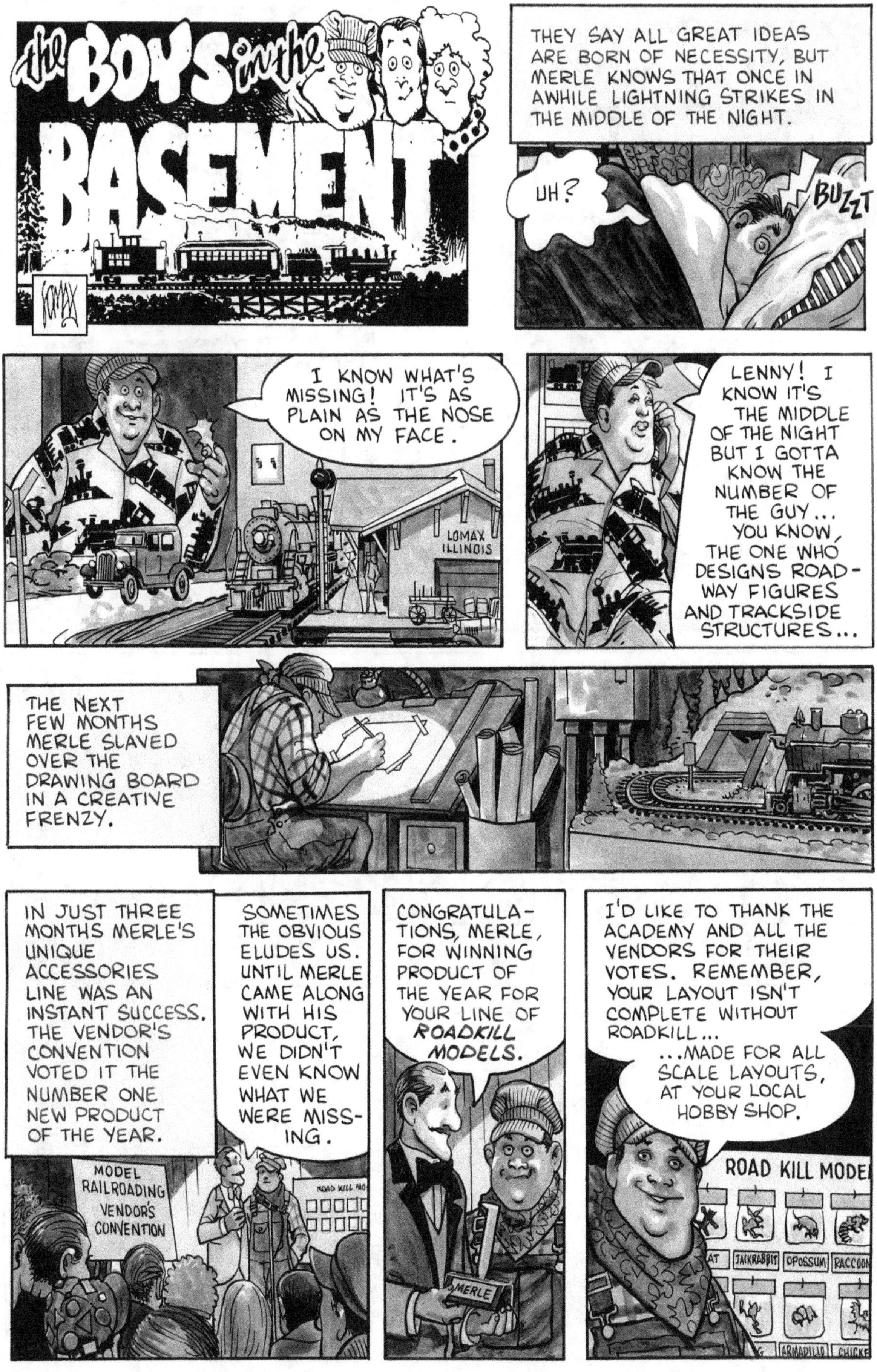
the BOYS in the BASEMENT
LOMAX
THEY SAY ALL GREAT IDEAS ARE BORN OF NECESSITY, BUT MERLE KNOWS THAT ONCE IN AWHILE LIGHTNING STRIKES IN THE MIDDLE OF THE NIGHT.
UH?
BUZZT
I KNOW WHAT'S MISSING! IT'S AS PLAIN AS THE NOSE ON MY FACE.
LOMAX ILLINOIS
LENNY! I KNOW IT'S THE MIDDLE OF THE NIGHT BUT I GOTTA KNOW THE NUMBER OF THE GUY... YOU KNOW, THE ONE WHO DESIGNS ROAD-WAY FIGURES AND TRACKSIDE STRUCTURES...
THE NEXT FEW MONTHS MERLE SLAVED OVER THE DRAWING BOARD IN A CREATIVE FRENZY.
IN JUST THREE MONTHS MERLE'S UNIQUE ACCESSORIES LINE WAS AN INSTANT SUCCESS. THE VENDOR'S CONVENTION VOTED IT THE NUMBER ONE NEW PRODUCT OF THE YEAR.
SOMETIMES THE OBVIOUS ELUDES US. UNTIL MERLE CAME ALONG WITH HIS PRODUCT, WE DIDN'T EVEN KNOW WHAT WE WERE MISS-ING.
MODEL RAILROADING VENDOR'S CONVENTION
CONGRATULA-TIONS, MERLE, FOR WINNING PRODUCT OF THE YEAR FOR YOUR LINE OF ROADKILL MODELS.
MERLE
I'D LIKE TO THANK THE ACADEMY AND ALL THE VENDORS FOR THEIR VOTES. REMEMBER, YOUR LAYOUT ISN'T COMPLETE WITHOUT ROADKILL...
...MADE FOR ALL SCALE LAYOUTS, AT YOUR LOCAL HOBBY SHOP.
JACKRABBIT
OPOSSUM
RACCOON
ARMADILLO

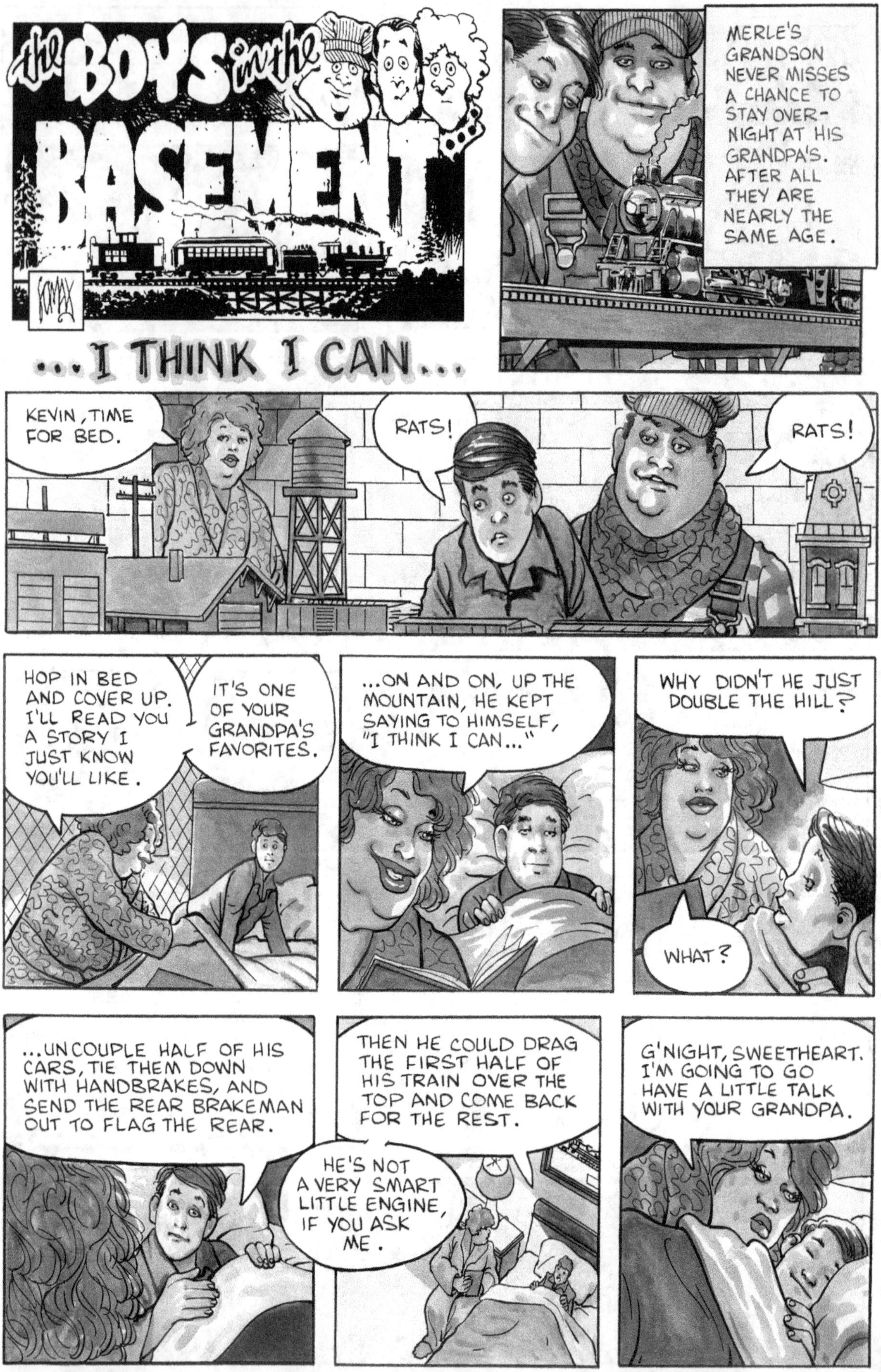
the BOYS in the BASEMENT
...I THINK I CAN...
MERLE'S GRANDSON NEVER MISSES A CHANCE TO STAY OVER-NIGHT AT HIS GRANDPA'S. AFTER ALL THEY ARE NEARLY THE SAME AGE.
KEVIN, TIME FOR BED.
RATS!
RATS!
HOP IN BED AND COVER UP. I'LL READ YOU A STORY I JUST KNOW YOU'LL LIKE.
IT'S ONE OF YOUR GRANDPA'S FAVORITES.
...ON AND ON, UP THE MOUNTAIN, HE KEPT SAYING TO HIMSELF, "I THINK I CAN..."
WHY DIDN'T HE JUST DOUBLE THE HILL?
WHAT?
...UNCOUPLE HALF OF HIS CARS, TIE THEM DOWN WITH HANDBRAKES, AND SEND THE REAR BRAKEMAN OUT TO FLAG THE REAR.
THEN HE COULD DRAG THE FIRST HALF OF HIS TRAIN OVER THE TOP AND COME BACK FOR THE REST.
HE'S NOT A VERY SMART LITTLE ENGINE, IF YOU ASK ME.
G'NIGHT, SWEETHEART. I'M GOING TO GO HAVE A LITTLE TALK WITH YOUR GRANDPA.

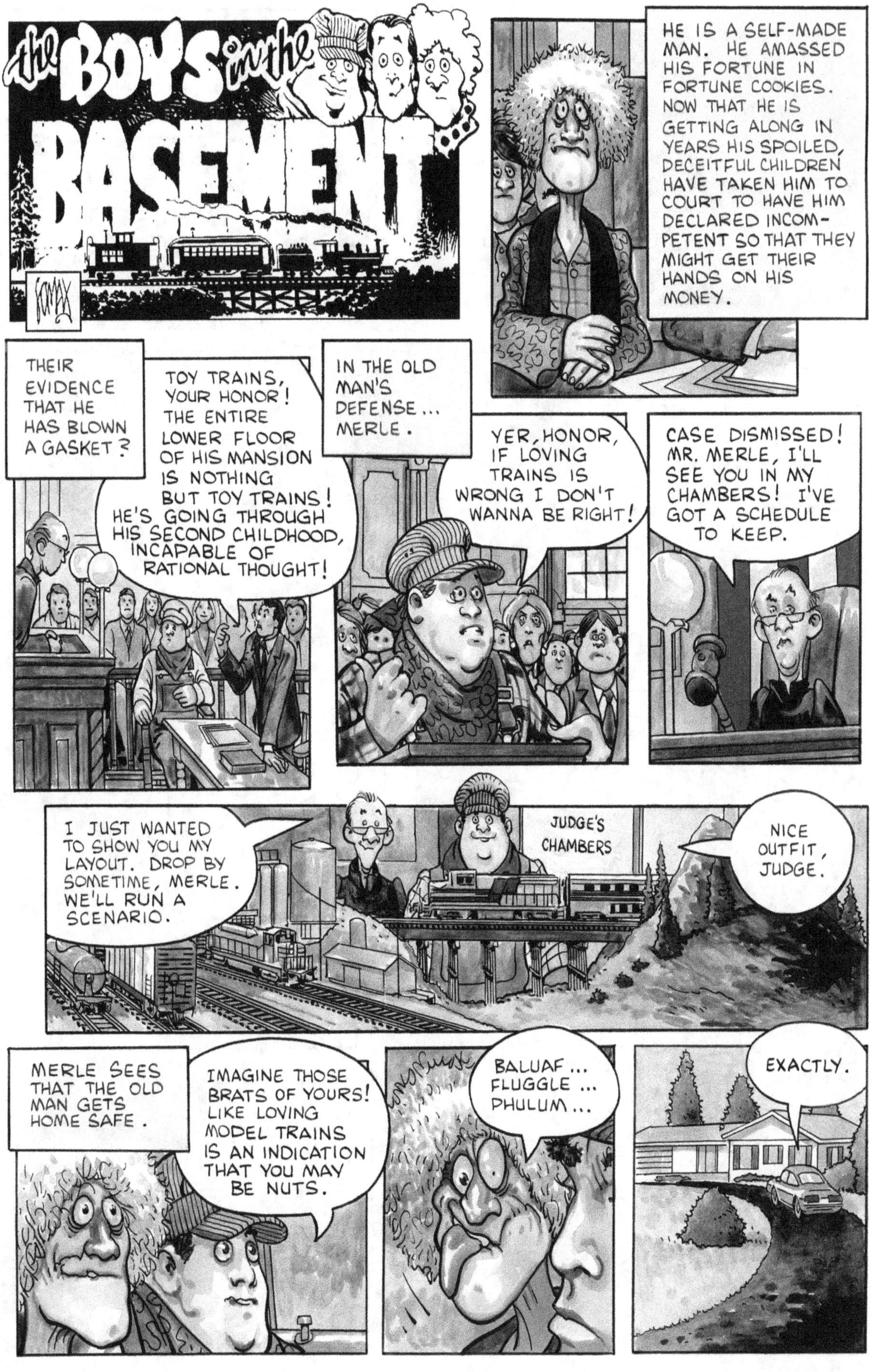
the BOYS in the BASEMENT
HE IS A SELF-MADE MAN. HE AMASSED HIS FORTUNE IN FORTUNE COOKIES. NOW THAT HE IS GETTING ALONG IN YEARS HIS SPOILED, DECEITFUL CHILDREN HAVE TAKEN HIM TO COURT TO HAVE HIM DECLARED INCOMPETENT SO THAT THEY MIGHT GET THEIR HANDS ON HIS MONEY.
THEIR EVIDENCE THAT HE HAS BLOWN A GASKET?
TOY TRAINS, YOUR HONOR! THE ENTIRE LOWER FLOOR OF HIS MANSION IS NOTHING BUT TOY TRAINS! HE'S GOING THROUGH HIS SECOND CHILDHOOD, INCAPABLE OF RATIONAL THOUGHT!
IN THE OLD MAN'S DEFENSE... MERLE.
YER, HONOR, IF LOVING TRAINS IS WRONG I DON'T WANNA BE RIGHT!
CASE DISMISSED! MR. MERLE, I'LL SEE YOU IN MY CHAMBERS! I'VE GOT A SCHEDULE TO KEEP.
I JUST WANTED TO SHOW YOU MY LAYOUT. DROP BY SOMETIME, MERLE. WE'LL RUN A SCENARIO.
JUDGE'S CHAMBERS
NICE OUTFIT, JUDGE.
MERLE SEES THAT THE OLD MAN GETS HOME SAFE.
IMAGINE THOSE BRATS OF YOURS! LIKE LOVING MODEL TRAINS IS AN INDICATION THAT YOU MAY BE NUTS.
BALUAF... FLUGGLE... PHULUM...
EXACTLY.

the BOYS in the BASEMENT
MERLE, WILL YOU WATCH AMY AND KEVIN WHILE WE GO TO THE STORE?
OH, SURE.
THIS WOULD BE A GOOD TIME TO GIVE YOU KIDS THE PRESENT GRANDPA GOT YOU.
BET IT HAS SOMETHING TO DO WITH TRAINS.
WHAT ELSE?
WOW! GRANDPA, THIS IS GREAT!
CAN WE SET IT UP TO PLAY?
MAINLINE EXPRESS
SURE, LET'S GO INTO THE LIVING ROOM.
MAINLINE EXPRES
THIS IS GONNA BE GREAT!
LATER...
I HOPE THE KIDS WEREN'T TOO MUCH FOR DAD ...
KIDS?
HI, MOM, WE'RE PLAYING "BIG ROCK CANDY MOUNTAIN", AND GRANDPA'S THE MOUNTAIN.
Z
Z
MUCH LATER ...
UH?
WELCOME BACK TO THE LAND OF THE LIVING, MERLE.

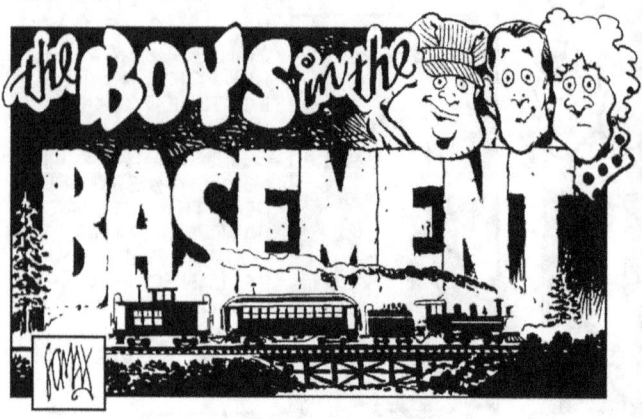

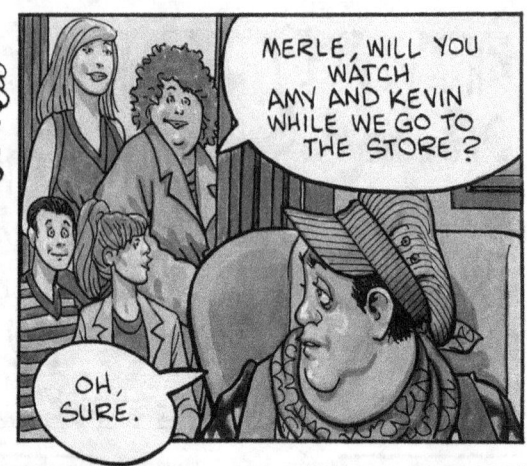

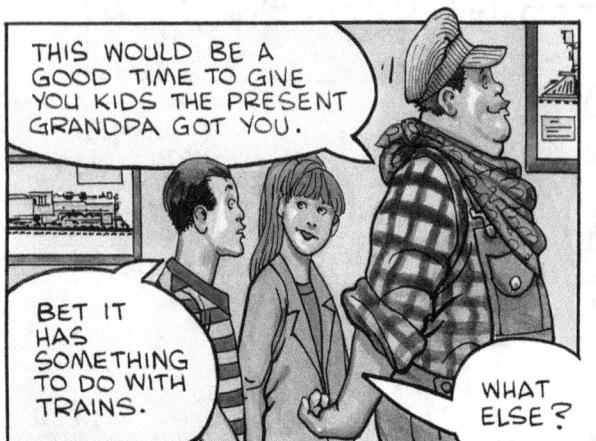

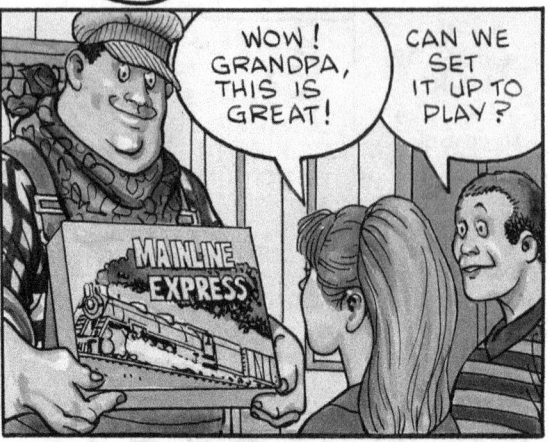

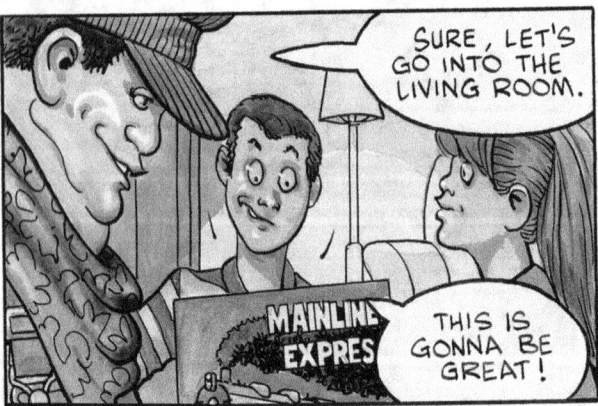

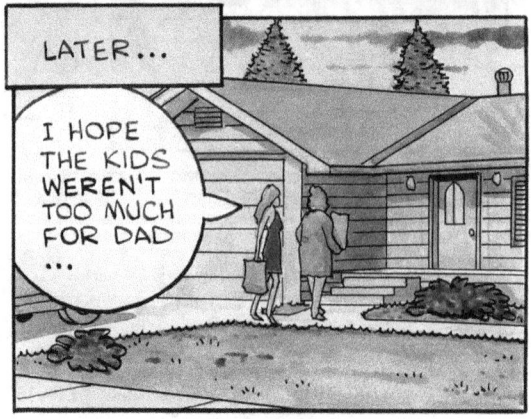

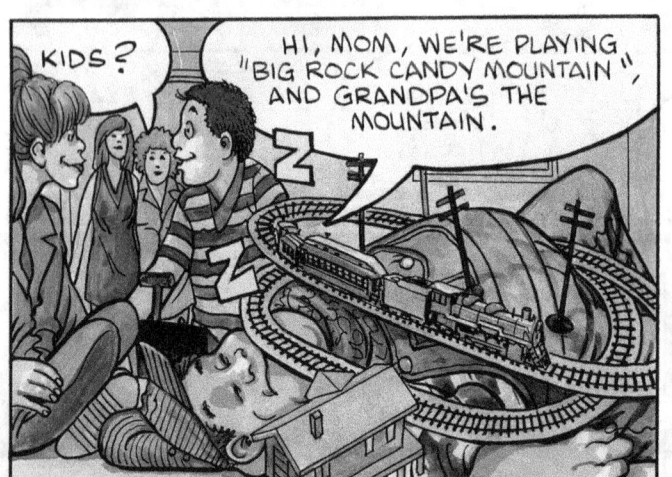

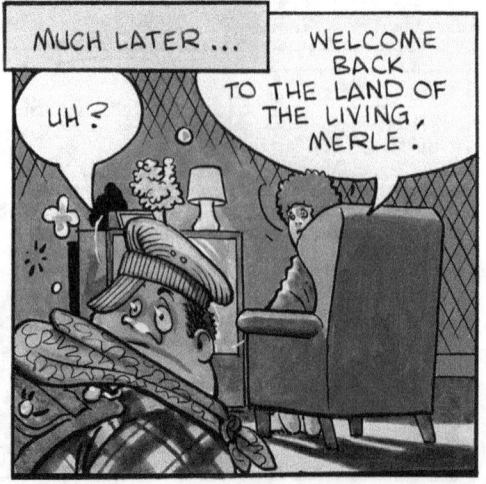

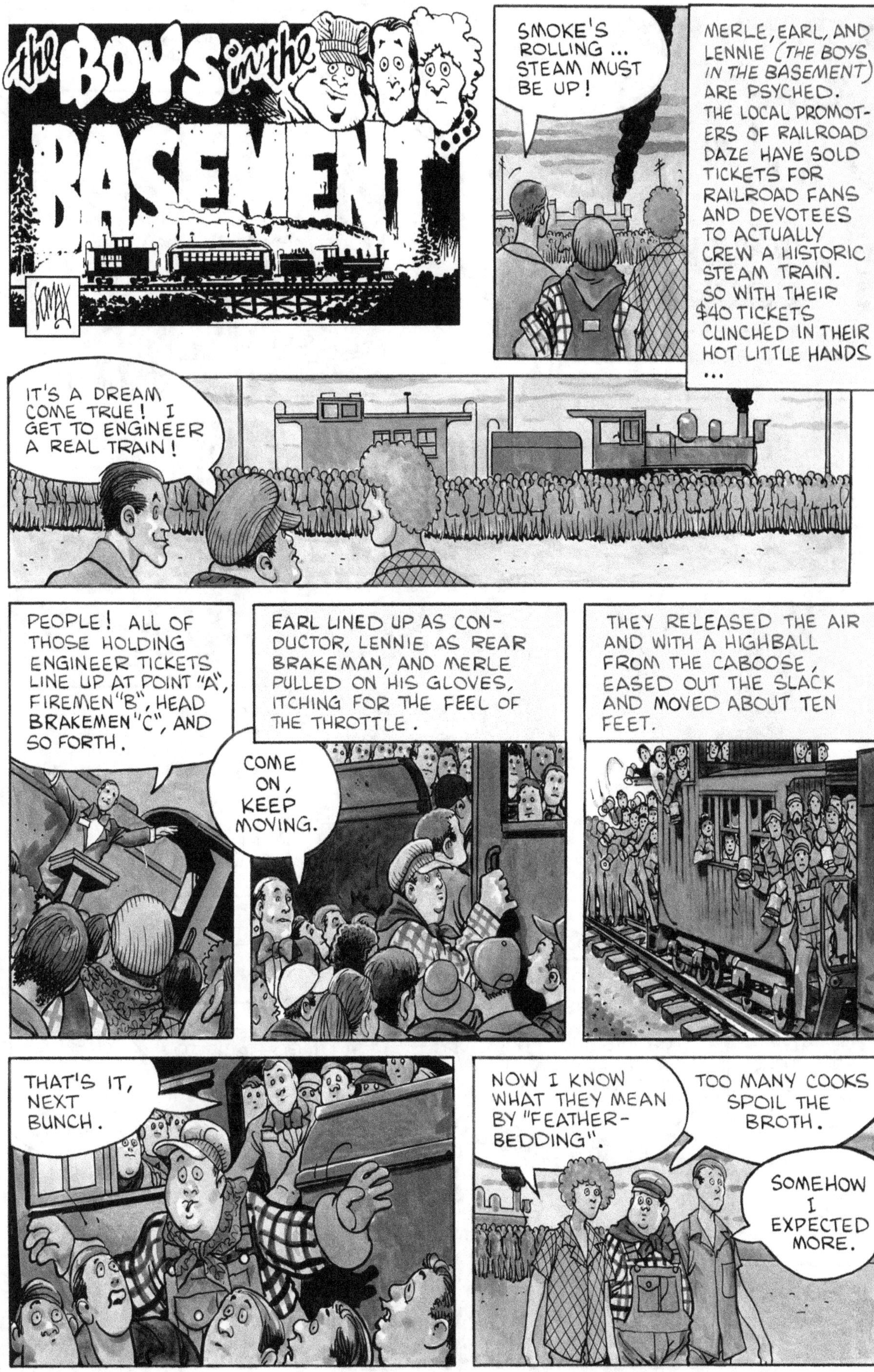
the BOYS in the BASEMENT
SOMAX
SMOKE'S ROLLING ... STEAM MUST BE UP!
MERLE, EARL, AND LENNIE (THE BOYS IN THE BASEMENT) ARE PSYCHED. THE LOCAL PROMOTERS OF RAILROAD DAZE HAVE SOLD TICKETS FOR RAILROAD FANS AND DEVOTEES TO ACTUALLY CREW A HISTORIC STEAM TRAIN. SO WITH THEIR $40 TICKETS CLINCHED IN THEIR HOT LITTLE HANDS ...
IT'S A DREAM COME TRUE! I GET TO ENGINEER A REAL TRAIN!
PEOPLE! ALL OF THOSE HOLDING ENGINEER TICKETS LINE UP AT POINT "A", FIREMEN "B", HEAD BRAKEMEN "C", AND SO FORTH.
EARL LINED UP AS CONDUCTOR, LENNIE AS REAR BRAKEMAN, AND MERLE PULLED ON HIS GLOVES, ITCHING FOR THE FEEL OF THE THROTTLE.
COME ON, KEEP MOVING.
THEY RELEASED THE AIR AND WITH A HIGHBALL FROM THE CABOOSE, EASED OUT THE SLACK AND MOVED ABOUT TEN FEET.
THAT'S IT, NEXT BUNCH.
NOW I KNOW WHAT THEY MEAN BY "FEATHER-BEDDING".
TOO MANY COOKS SPOIL THE BROTH.
SOMEHOW I EXPECTED MORE.

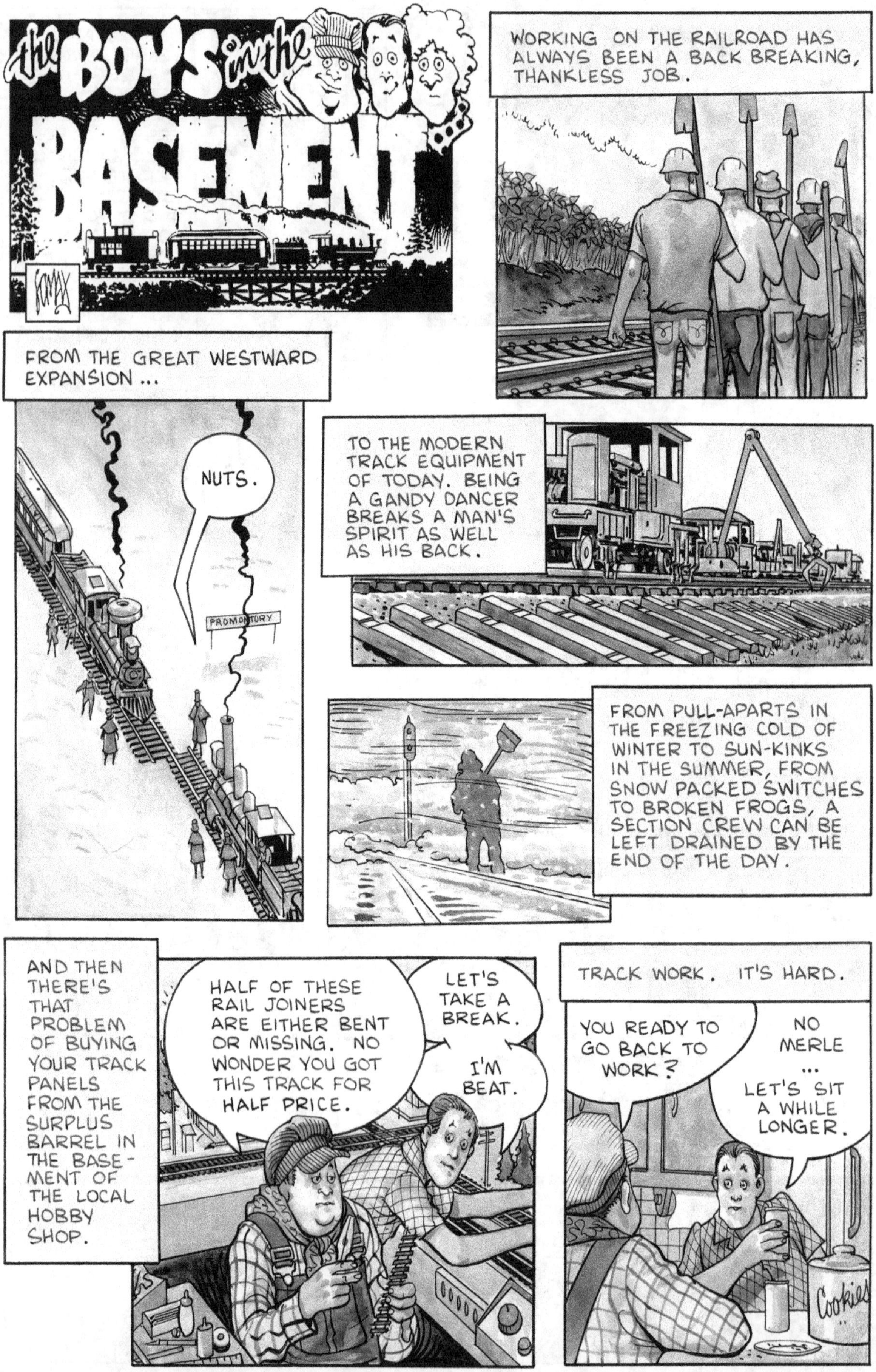
the BOYS in the BASEMENT
WORKING ON THE RAILROAD HAS ALWAYS BEEN A BACK BREAKING, THANKLESS JOB.
FROM THE GREAT WESTWARD EXPANSION ...
NUTS.
PROMONTORY
TO THE MODERN TRACK EQUIPMENT OF TODAY. BEING A GANDY DANCER BREAKS A MAN'S SPIRIT AS WELL AS HIS BACK.
FROM PULL-APARTS IN THE FREEZING COLD OF WINTER TO SUN-KINKS IN THE SUMMER, FROM SNOW PACKED SWITCHES TO BROKEN FROGS, A SECTION CREW CAN BE LEFT DRAINED BY THE END OF THE DAY.
AND THEN THERE'S THAT PROBLEM OF BUYING YOUR TRACK PANELS FROM THE SURPLUS BARREL IN THE BASE-MENT OF THE LOCAL HOBBY SHOP.
HALF OF THESE RAIL JOINERS ARE EITHER BENT OR MISSING. NO WONDER YOU GOT THIS TRACK FOR HALF PRICE.
LET'S TAKE A BREAK.
I'M BEAT.
TRACK WORK. IT'S HARD.
YOU READY TO GO BACK TO WORK?
NO MERLE ... LET'S SIT A WHILE LONGER.
Cookies

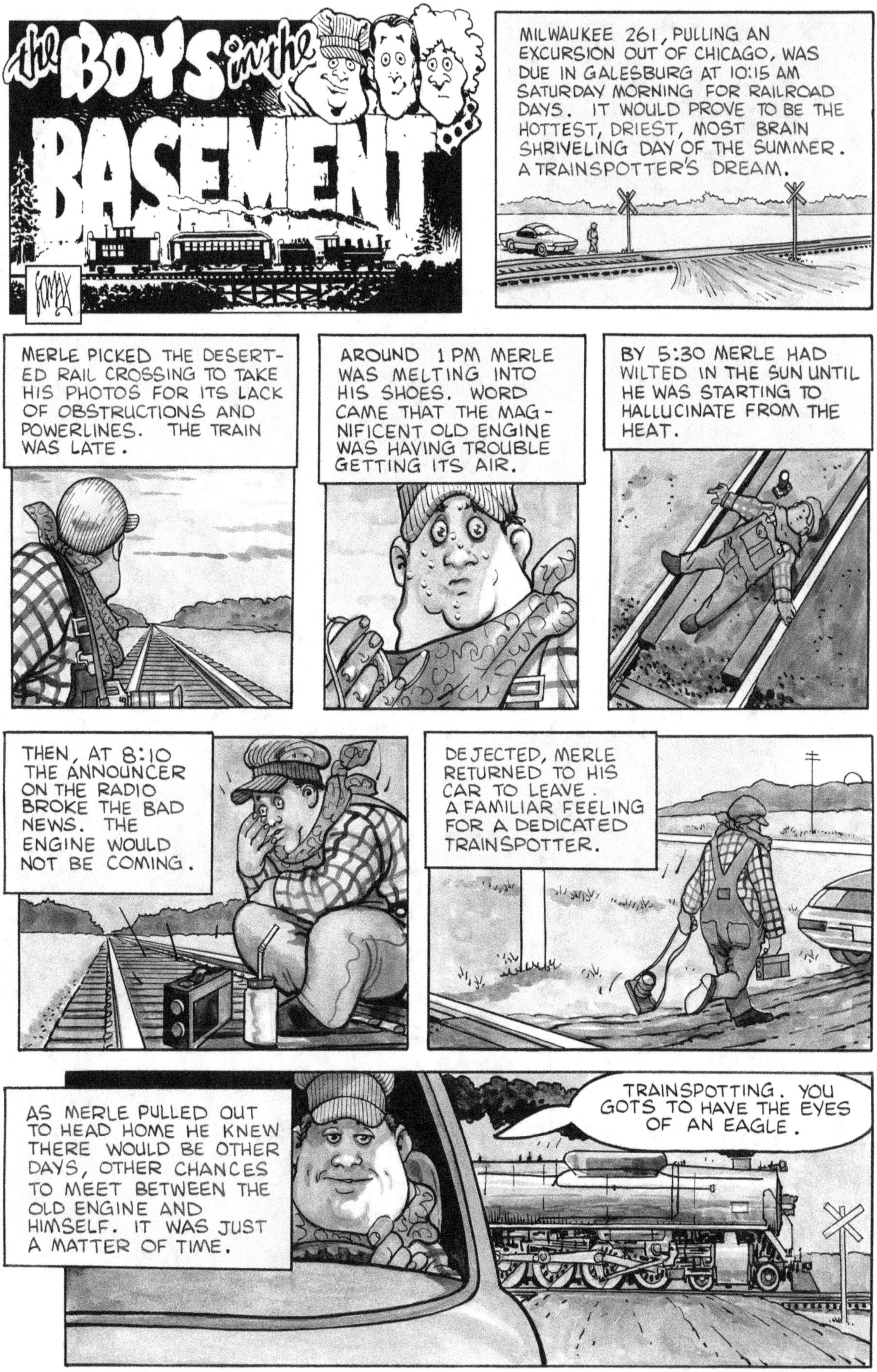
the BOYS in the BASEMENT
MILWAUKEE 261, PULLING AN EXCURSION OUT OF CHICAGO, WAS DUE IN GALESBURG AT 10:15 AM SATURDAY MORNING FOR RAILROAD DAYS. IT WOULD PROVE TO BE THE HOTTEST, DRIEST, MOST BRAIN SHRIVELING DAY OF THE SUMMER. A TRAINSPOTTER'S DREAM.
MERLE PICKED THE DESERTED RAIL CROSSING TO TAKE HIS PHOTOS FOR ITS LACK OF OBSTRUCTIONS AND POWERLINES. THE TRAIN WAS LATE.
AROUND 1 PM MERLE WAS MELTING INTO HIS SHOES. WORD CAME THAT THE MAGNIFICENT OLD ENGINE WAS HAVING TROUBLE GETTING ITS AIR.
BY 5:30 MERLE HAD WILTED IN THE SUN UNTIL HE WAS STARTING TO HALLUCINATE FROM THE HEAT.
THEN, AT 8:10 THE ANNOUNCER ON THE RADIO BROKE THE BAD NEWS. THE ENGINE WOULD NOT BE COMING.
DEJECTED, MERLE RETURNED TO HIS CAR TO LEAVE. A FAMILIAR FEELING FOR A DEDICATED TRAINSPOTTER.
AS MERLE PULLED OUT TO HEAD HOME HE KNEW THERE WOULD BE OTHER DAYS, OTHER CHANCES TO MEET BETWEEN THE OLD ENGINE AND HIMSELF. IT WAS JUST A MATTER OF TIME.
TRAINSPOTTING. YOU GOTS TO HAVE THE EYES OF AN EAGLE.

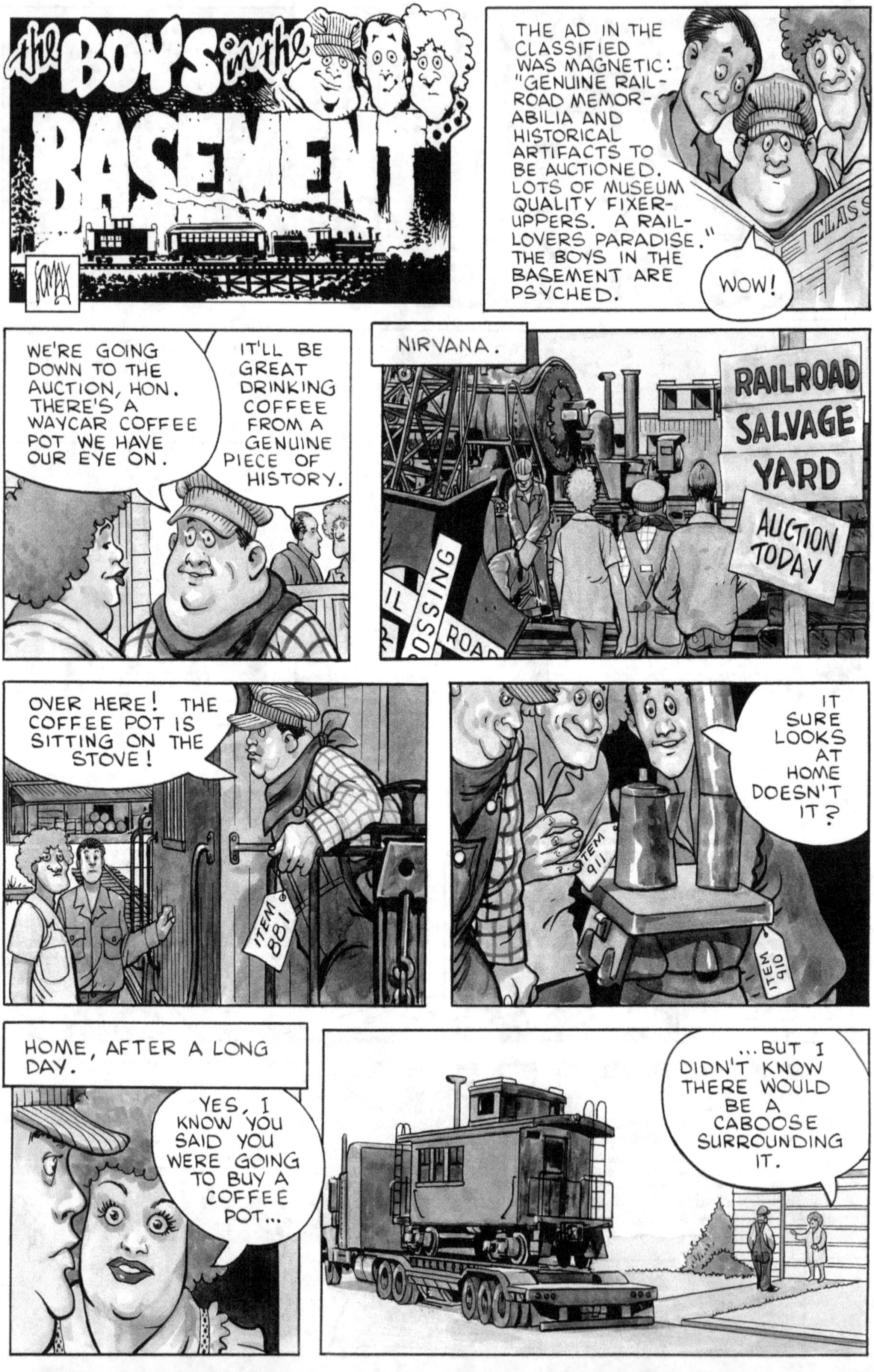
the BOYS in the BASEMENT
THE AD IN THE CLASSIFIED WAS MAGNETIC: "GENUINE RAIL-ROAD MEMOR-ABILIA AND HISTORICAL ARTIFACTS TO BE AUCTIONED. LOTS OF MUSEUM QUALITY FIXER-UPPERS. A RAIL-LOVERS PARADISE." THE BOYS IN THE BASEMENT ARE PSYCHED.
WOW!
CLASS
WE'RE GOING DOWN TO THE AUCTION, HON. THERE'S A WAYCAR COFFEE POT WE HAVE OUR EYE ON.
IT'LL BE GREAT DRINKING COFFEE FROM A GENUINE PIECE OF HISTORY.
NIRVANA.
RAILROAD SALVAGE YARD
AUCTION TODAY
OSSING
ROAD
OVER HERE! THE COFFEE POT IS SITTING ON THE STOVE!
ITEM 881
IT SURE LOOKS AT HOME DOESN'T IT?
ITEM 911
ITEM 910
HOME, AFTER A LONG DAY.
YES, I KNOW YOU SAID YOU WERE GOING TO BUY A COFFEE POT...
...BUT I DIDN'T KNOW THERE WOULD BE A CABOOSE SURROUNDING IT.

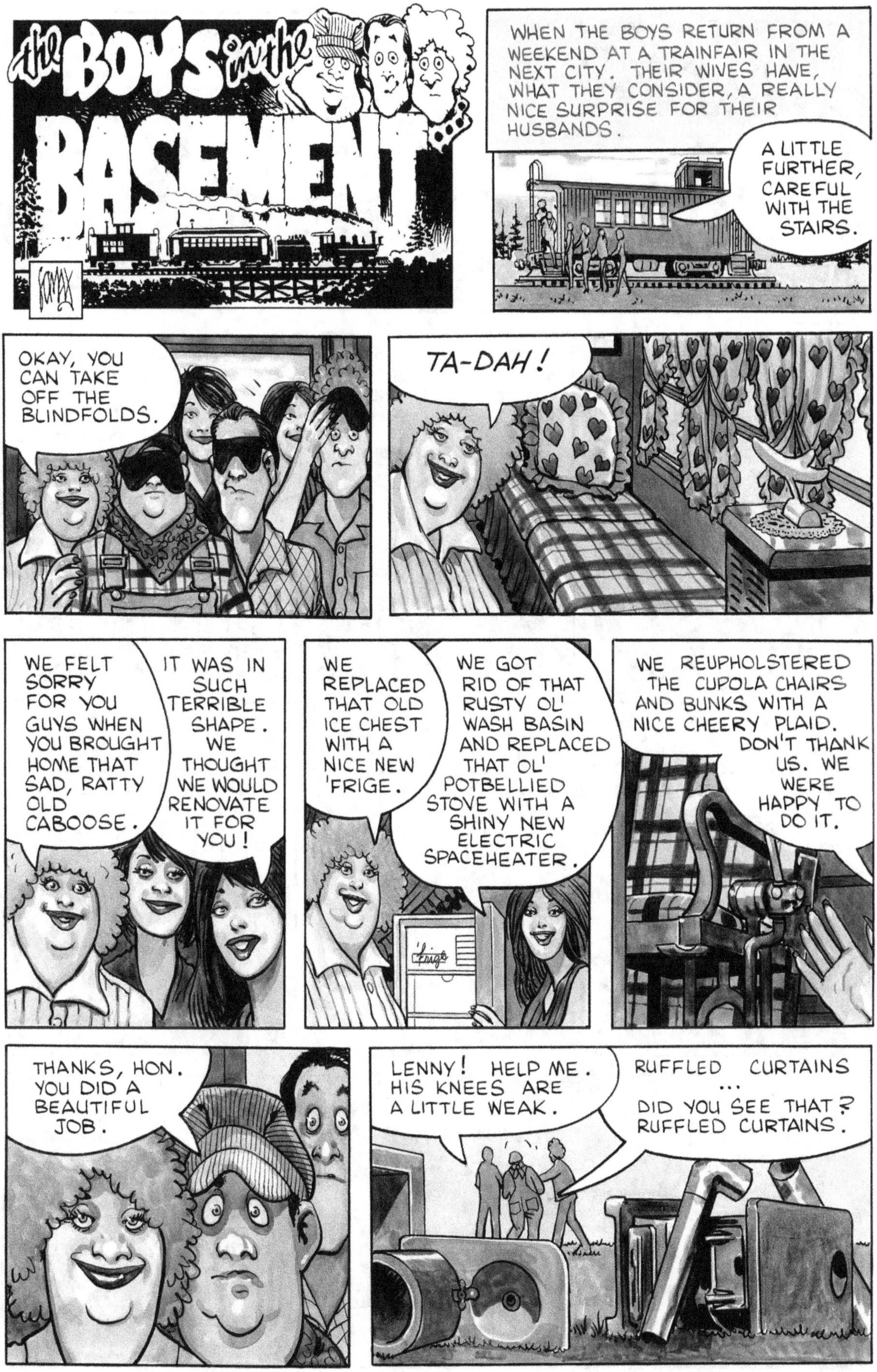

the BOYS in the BASEMENT
WHEN THE BOYS RETURN FROM A WEEKEND AT A TRAINFAIR IN THE NEXT CITY. THEIR WIVES HAVE, WHAT THEY CONSIDER, A REALLY NICE SURPRISE FOR THEIR HUSBANDS.
A LITTLE FURTHER, CAREFUL WITH THE STAIRS.
OKAY, YOU CAN TAKE OFF THE BLINDFOLDS.
TA-DAH!
WE FELT SORRY FOR YOU GUYS WHEN YOU BROUGHT HOME THAT SAD, RATTY OLD CABOOSE.
IT WAS IN SUCH TERRIBLE SHAPE. WE THOUGHT WE WOULD RENOVATE IT FOR YOU!
WE REPLACED THAT OLD ICE CHEST WITH A NICE NEW 'FRIGE.
WE GOT RID OF THAT RUSTY OL' WASH BASIN AND REPLACED THAT OL' POTBELLIED STOVE WITH A SHINY NEW ELECTRIC SPACEHEATER.
WE REUPHOLSTERED THE CUPOLA CHAIRS AND BUNKS WITH A NICE CHEERY PLAID.
DON'T THANK US. WE WERE HAPPY TO DO IT.
THANKS, HON. YOU DID A BEAUTIFUL JOB.
LENNY! HELP ME. HIS KNEES ARE A LITTLE WEAK.
RUFFLED CURTAINS ... DID YOU SEE THAT? RUFFLED CURTAINS.

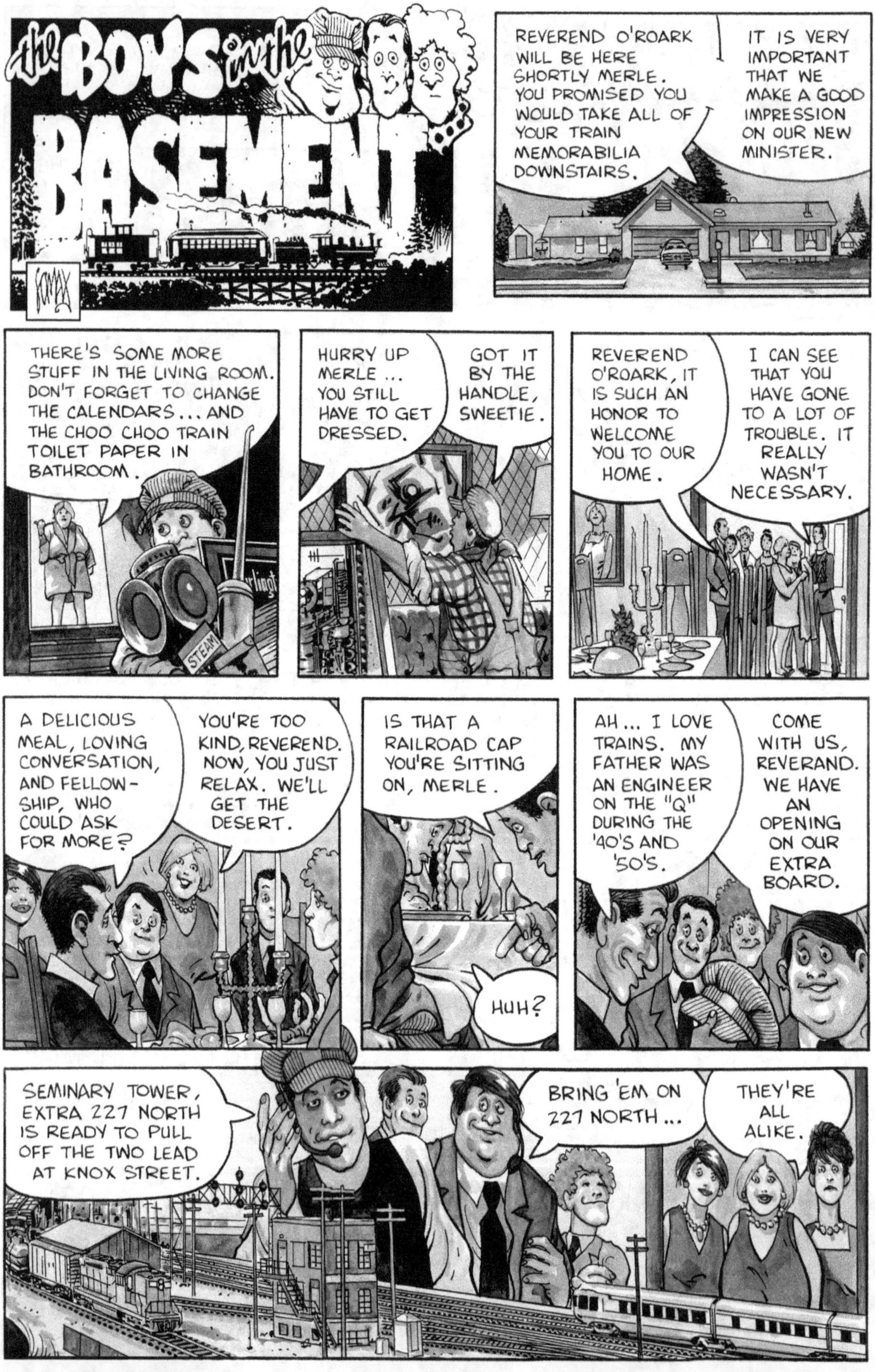
the BOYS in the BASEMENT
REVEREND O'ROARK WILL BE HERE SHORTLY MERLE. YOU PROMISED YOU WOULD TAKE ALL OF YOUR TRAIN MEMORABILIA DOWNSTAIRS.
IT IS VERY IMPORTANT THAT WE MAKE A GOOD IMPRESSION ON OUR NEW MINISTER.
THERE'S SOME MORE STUFF IN THE LIVING ROOM. DON'T FORGET TO CHANGE THE CALENDARS... AND THE CHOO CHOO TRAIN TOILET PAPER IN BATHROOM.
STEAM
HURRY UP MERLE ... YOU STILL HAVE TO GET DRESSED.
GOT IT BY THE HANDLE, SWEETIE.
REVEREND O'ROARK, IT IS SUCH AN HONOR TO WELCOME YOU TO OUR HOME.
I CAN SEE THAT YOU HAVE GONE TO A LOT OF TROUBLE. IT REALLY WASN'T NECESSARY.
A DELICIOUS MEAL, LOVING CONVERSATION, AND FELLOW-SHIP, WHO COULD ASK FOR MORE?
YOU'RE TOO KIND, REVEREND. NOW, YOU JUST RELAX. WE'LL GET THE DESERT.
IS THAT A RAILROAD CAP YOU'RE SITTING ON, MERLE.
HUH?
AH ... I LOVE TRAINS. MY FATHER WAS AN ENGINEER ON THE "Q" DURING THE '40'S AND '50'S.
COME WITH US, REVERAND. WE HAVE AN OPENING ON OUR EXTRA BOARD.
SEMINARY TOWER, EXTRA 227 NORTH IS READY TO PULL OFF THE TWO LEAD AT KNOX STREET.
BRING 'EM ON 227 NORTH ...
THEY'RE ALL ALIKE.

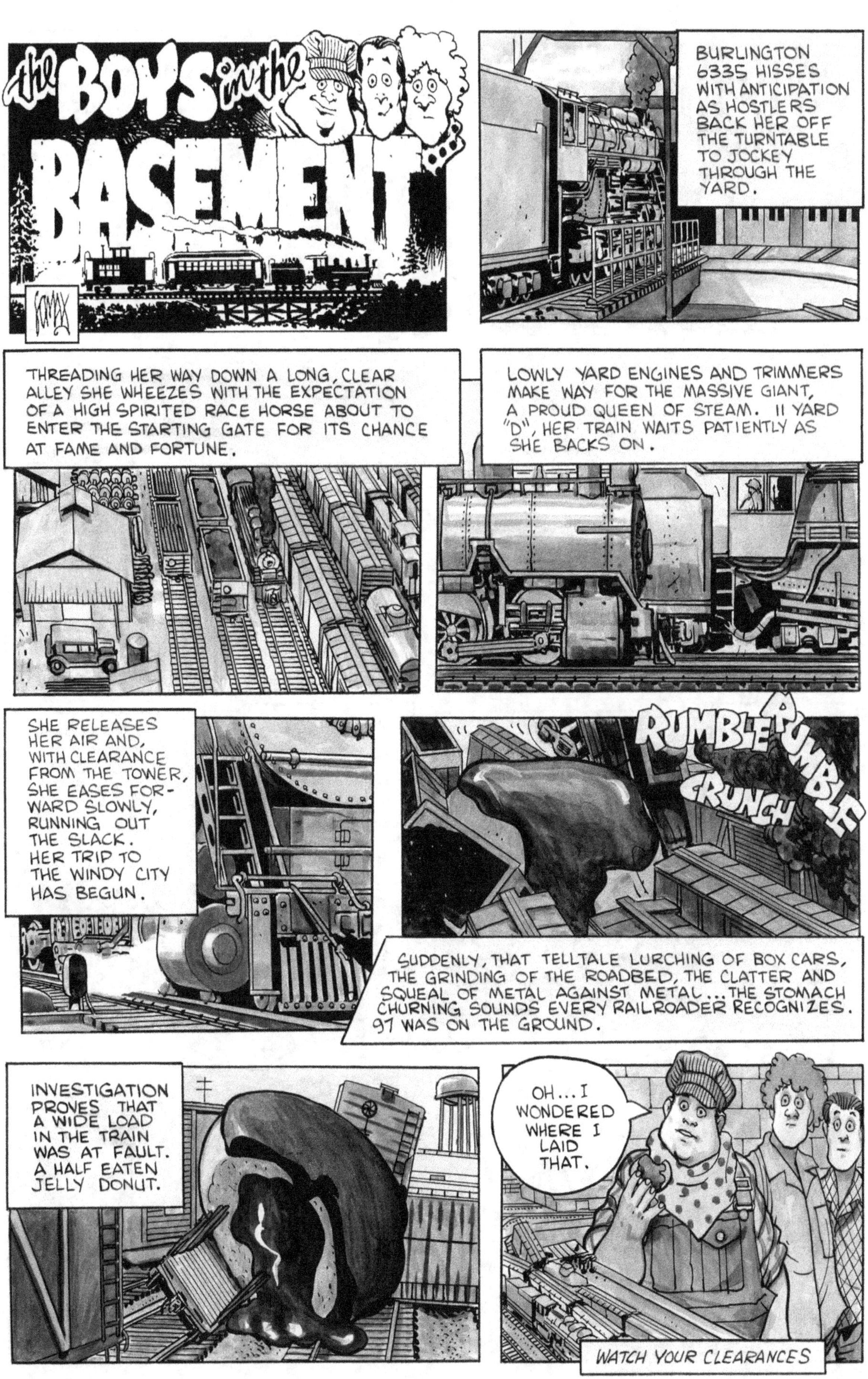

the BOYS in the BASEMENT
BURLINGTON 6335 HISSES WITH ANTICIPATION AS HOSTLERS BACK HER OFF THE TURNTABLE TO JOCKEY THROUGH THE YARD.
THREADING HER WAY DOWN A LONG, CLEAR ALLEY SHE WHEEZES WITH THE EXPECTATION OF A HIGH SPIRITED RACE HORSE ABOUT TO ENTER THE STARTING GATE FOR ITS CHANCE AT FAME AND FORTUNE.
LOWLY YARD ENGINES AND TRIMMERS MAKE WAY FOR THE MASSIVE GIANT, A PROUD QUEEN OF STEAM. 11 YARD "D", HER TRAIN WAITS PATIENTLY AS SHE BACKS ON.
SHE RELEASES HER AIR AND, WITH CLEARANCE FROM THE TOWER, SHE EASES FOR-WARD SLOWLY, RUNNING OUT THE SLACK. HER TRIP TO THE WINDY CITY HAS BEGUN.
RUMBLE RUMBLE RUMBLE
CRUNCH
SUDDENLY, THAT TELLTALE LURCHING OF BOX CARS, THE GRINDING OF THE ROADBED, THE CLATTER AND SQUEAL OF METAL AGAINST METAL... THE STOMACH CHURNING SOUNDS EVERY RAILROADER RECOGNIZES. 97 WAS ON THE GROUND.
INVESTIGATION PROVES THAT A WIDE LOAD IN THE TRAIN WAS AT FAULT. A HALF EATEN JELLY DONUT.
OH... I WONDERED WHERE I LAID THAT.
WATCH YOUR CLEARANCES

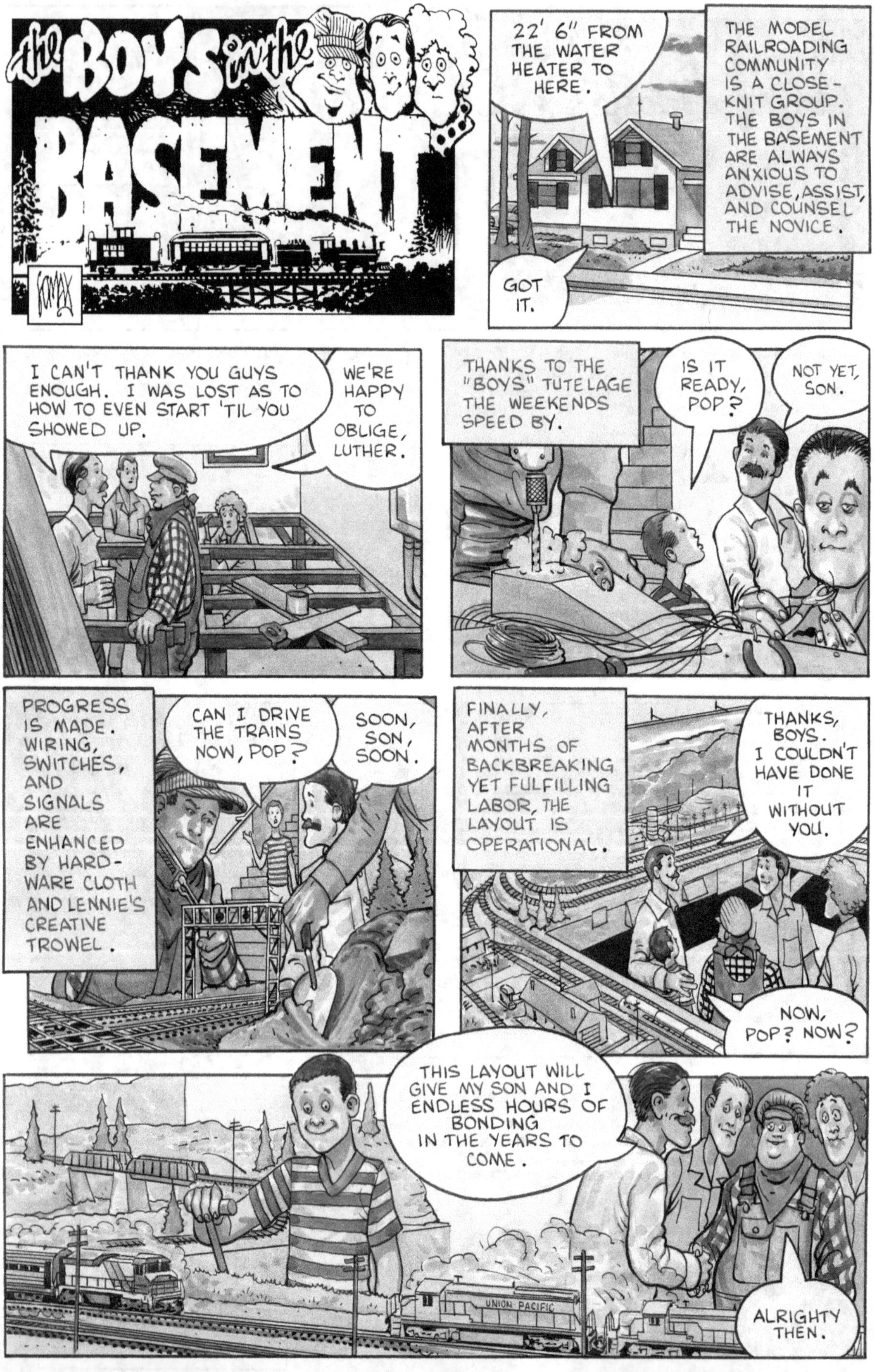
the BOYS in the BASEMENT
22' 6" FROM THE WATER HEATER TO HERE.
GOT IT.
THE MODEL RAILROADING COMMUNITY IS A CLOSE-KNIT GROUP. THE BOYS IN THE BASEMENT ARE ALWAYS ANXIOUS TO ADVISE, ASSIST, AND COUNSEL THE NOVICE.
I CAN'T THANK YOU GUYS ENOUGH. I WAS LOST AS TO HOW TO EVEN START 'TIL YOU SHOWED UP.
WE'RE HAPPY TO OBLIGE, LUTHER.
THANKS TO THE "BOYS" TUTELAGE THE WEEKENDS SPEED BY.
IS IT READY, POP?
NOT YET, SON.
PROGRESS IS MADE. WIRING, SWITCHES, AND SIGNALS ARE ENHANCED BY HARD-WARE CLOTH AND LENNIE'S CREATIVE TROWEL.
CAN I DRIVE THE TRAINS NOW, POP?
SOON, SON, SOON.
FINALLY, AFTER MONTHS OF BACKBREAKING YET FULFILLING LABOR, THE LAYOUT IS OPERATIONAL.
THANKS, BOYS. I COULDN'T HAVE DONE IT WITHOUT YOU.
NOW, POP? NOW?
THIS LAYOUT WILL GIVE MY SON AND I ENDLESS HOURS OF BONDING IN THE YEARS TO COME.
UNION PACIFIC
ALRIGHTY THEN.

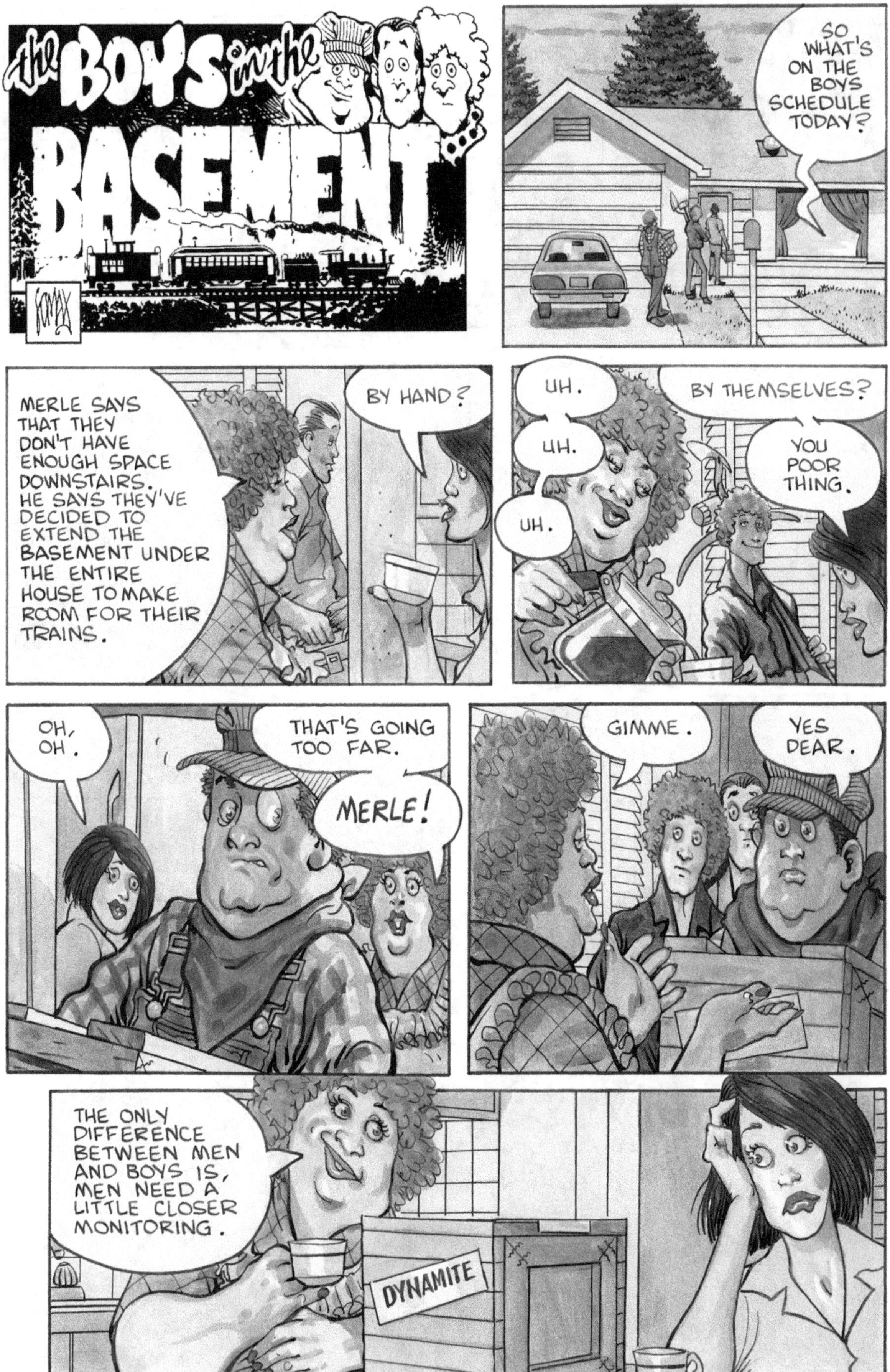
the BOYS in the BASEMENT
SO WHAT'S ON THE BOYS SCHEDULE TODAY?
MERLE SAYS THAT THEY DON'T HAVE ENOUGH SPACE DOWNSTAIRS. HE SAYS THEY'VE DECIDED TO EXTEND THE BASEMENT UNDER THE ENTIRE HOUSE TO MAKE ROOM FOR THEIR TRAINS.
BY HAND?
UH.
UH.
UH.
BY THEMSELVES?
YOU POOR THING.
OH, OH.
THAT'S GOING TOO FAR.
MERLE!
GIMME.
YES DEAR.
THE ONLY DIFFERENCE BETWEEN MEN AND BOYS IS, MEN NEED A LITTLE CLOSER MONITORING.
DYNAMITE

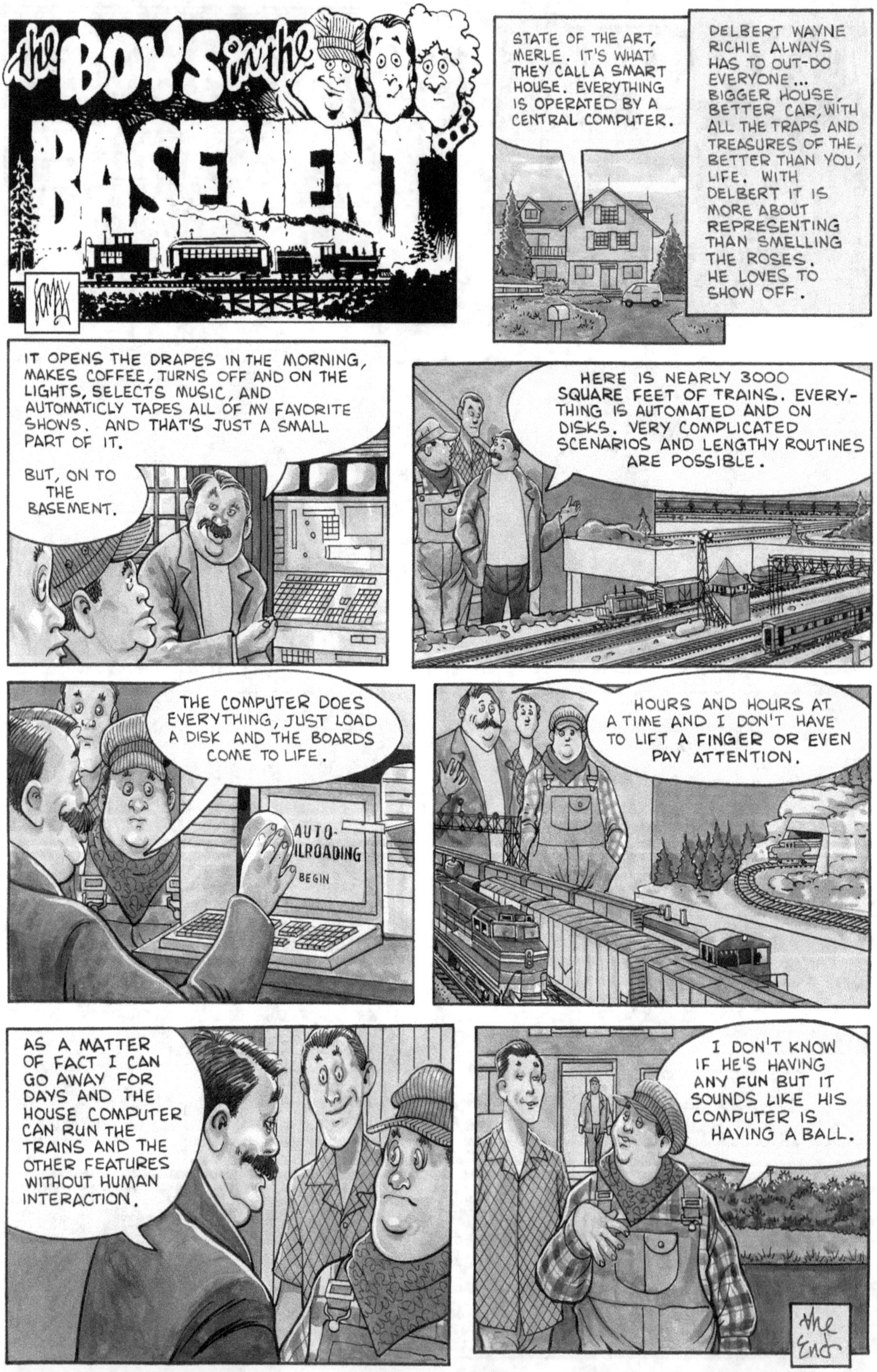

the BOYS in the BASEMENT
STATE OF THE ART, MERLE. IT'S WHAT THEY CALL A SMART HOUSE. EVERYTHING IS OPERATED BY A CENTRAL COMPUTER.
DELBERT WAYNE RICHIE ALWAYS HAS TO OUT-DO EVERYONE... BIGGER HOUSE, BETTER CAR, WITH ALL THE TRAPS AND TREASURES OF THE, BETTER THAN YOU, LIFE. WITH DELBERT IT IS MORE ABOUT REPRESENTING THAN SMELLING THE ROSES. HE LOVES TO SHOW OFF.
IT OPENS THE DRAPES IN THE MORNING, MAKES COFFEE, TURNS OFF AND ON THE LIGHTS, SELECTS MUSIC, AND AUTOMATICLY TAPES ALL OF MY FAVORITE SHOWS. AND THAT'S JUST A SMALL PART OF IT.
BUT, ON TO THE BASEMENT.
HERE IS NEARLY 3000 SQUARE FEET OF TRAINS. EVERY-THING IS AUTOMATED AND ON DISKS. VERY COMPLICATED SCENARIOS AND LENGTHY ROUTINES ARE POSSIBLE.
THE COMPUTER DOES EVERYTHING, JUST LOAD A DISK AND THE BOARDS COME TO LIFE.
AUTO-
ILROADING
BEGIN
HOURS AND HOURS AT A TIME AND I DON'T HAVE TO LIFT A FINGER OR EVEN PAY ATTENTION.
AS A MATTER OF FACT I CAN GO AWAY FOR DAYS AND THE HOUSE COMPUTER CAN RUN THE TRAINS AND THE OTHER FEATURES WITHOUT HUMAN INTERACTION.
I DON'T KNOW IF HE'S HAVING ANY FUN BUT IT SOUNDS LIKE HIS COMPUTER IS HAVING A BALL.
the End

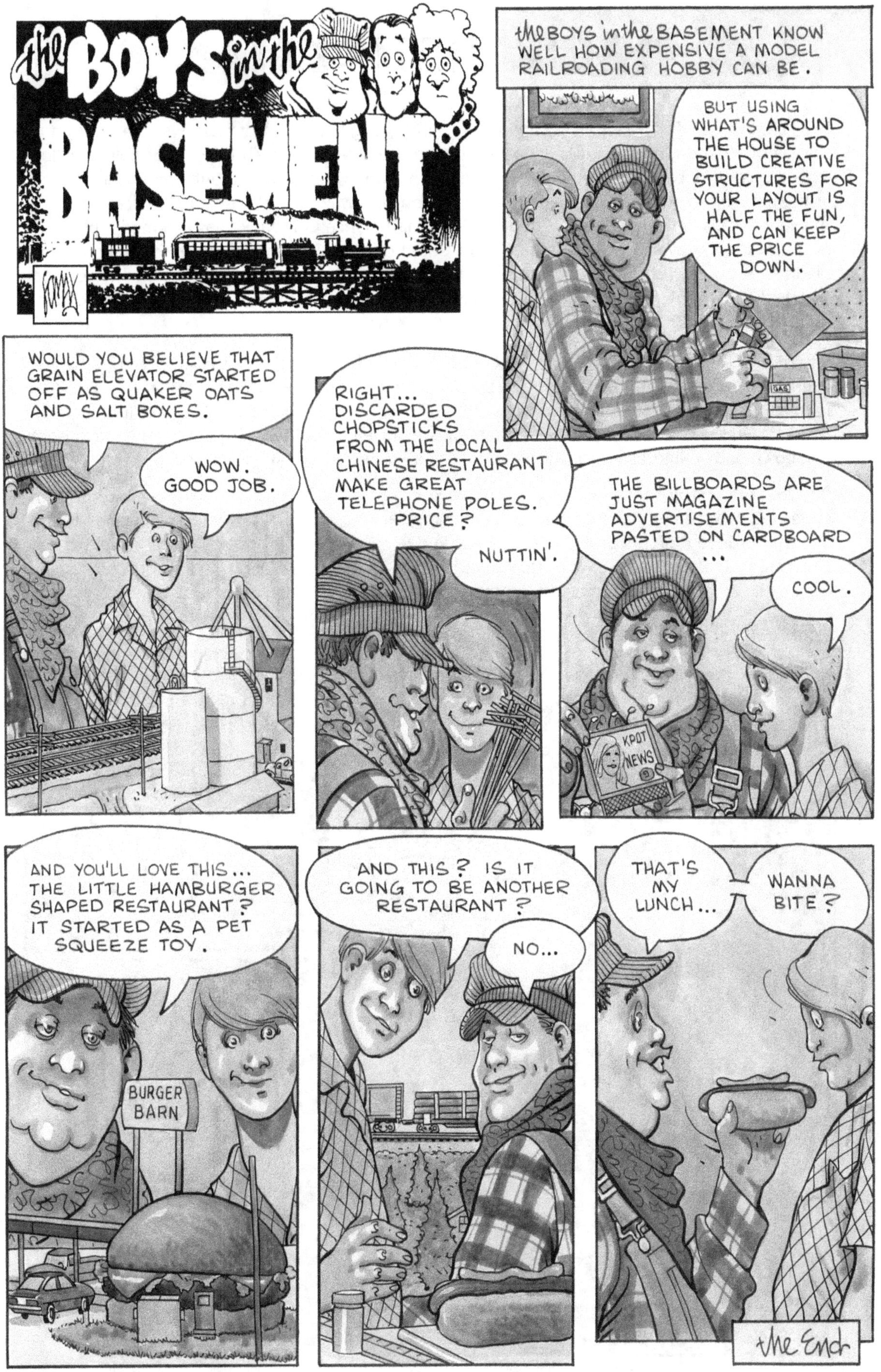
the BOYS in the BASEMENT
the BOYS in the BASEMENT KNOW WELL HOW EXPENSIVE A MODEL RAILROADING HOBBY CAN BE.
BUT USING WHAT'S AROUND THE HOUSE TO BUILD CREATIVE STRUCTURES FOR YOUR LAYOUT IS HALF THE FUN, AND CAN KEEP THE PRICE DOWN.
GAS
WOULD YOU BELIEVE THAT GRAIN ELEVATOR STARTED OFF AS QUAKER OATS AND SALT BOXES.
WOW. GOOD JOB.
RIGHT... DISCARDED CHOPSTICKS FROM THE LOCAL CHINESE RESTAURANT MAKE GREAT TELEPHONE POLES. PRICE?
NUTTIN'.
THE BILLBOARDS ARE JUST MAGAZINE ADVERTISEMENTS PASTED ON CARDBOARD...
COOL.
KPDT NEWS
AND YOU'LL LOVE THIS... THE LITTLE HAMBURGER SHAPED RESTAURANT? IT STARTED AS A PET SQUEEZE TOY.
BURGER BARN
AND THIS? IS IT GOING TO BE ANOTHER RESTAURANT?
NO...
THAT'S MY LUNCH...
WANNA BITE?
the End

ABOUT DON LOMAX

DON LOMAX was drafted into the Army in 1965 and, along with most draftees went to Vietnam in the fall of 1966 during President Johnson's targeted build-up to reach his goal of half a million troops in-country by the summer of 1967. Being an orphan company without a particular mission at the time, upon arriving in the Cha Rang Valley on Highway 19 in the near geological center of the country, his unit (the 98th Light Equipment Maintenance Company) was assigned a plethora of duties from convoying supplies, to airport guard duty at Qui Nhon Airport, to repairing Fuel bladders, with a little shit burning thrown in for fun. All the while he took mental notes and sketched the people, the gear, and the countryside thinking, "This would make a great comic." And it did.

VIETNAM JOURNAL, the comic book was first published by Apple Publishing in 1987 and was eventually nominated for a Harvey Award. He has had a long career now approaching 50 years in magazine and comic books including a stint at writing The 'Nam and The Punisher for Marvel in the '90s. Other spin-offs, High Shining Brass, Valley of Death, and Tet '68 are still available in print and download on-line, as well as the Vietnam Journal series from Caliber Comics.

But Don Lomax is by no means a one trick pony. For nearly 50 years he has had comics and cartoons appearing in a score of national magazines on a regular basis including Easyrider, CARtoons, Heavy Metal, Overdrive (Knights of the Road), Police and Security News (Above and Beyond), American Towman, and many others. But he also worked for most of the major comic book imprints including Pacific, Marvel, First, Americomics, Fantagraphics,Transfuzion, Eros and of course Caliber.

Lomax has four great children, two girls and two boys with ten grandchildren, and twelve great grandchildren (at last count). His sons are both veterans, his oldest Bryan served in Panama during operation Just Cause and Torrin with the Special Forces during several tours in Iraq and Afghanistan. Both are retired now. Lomax now lives in Illinois with the light of his life, his wife, Zenaida and is hard at work on Series Two of Vietnam Journal. (well, not THAT hard at work. When you love what you do it can't really be called work, can it?)

CALIBER COMICS PRESENTS
The Complete
VIETNAM JOURNAL

  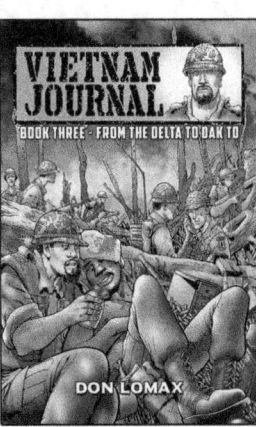 

8 Volumes Covering the Entire Initial Run of the Critically Acclaimed Don Lomax Series

And Now Available
VIETNAM JOURNAL SERIES TWO
"INCURSION", "JOURNEY INTO HELL", "RIPCORD"

All new stories from Scott 'Journal' Neithammer as he reports durings the later stages of the Vietnam War.

FROM CALIBER COMICS
www.calibercomics.com

ALSO AVAILABLE FROM DON LOMAX

HIGH SHINING BRASS

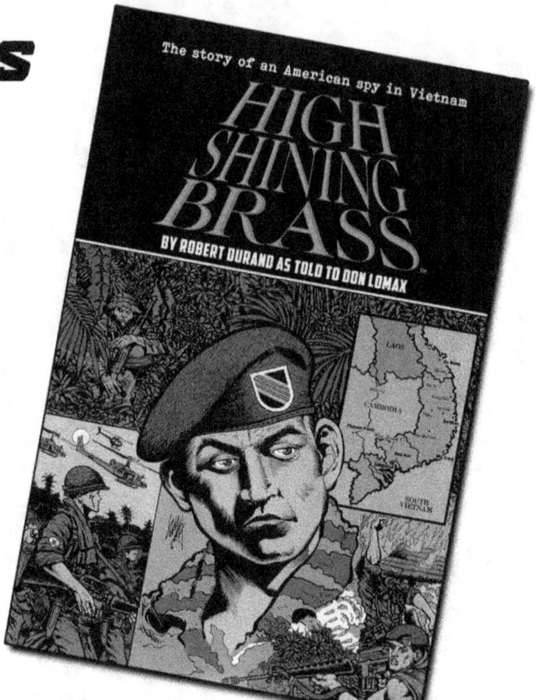
The story of an American spy in Vietnam
HIGH SHINING BRASS
BY ROBERT DURAND AS TOLD TO DON LOMAX

High Shining Brass is based on the true story of an American spy during the Vietnam War as told to Don Lomax by agent Robert Durand who chronicles the tale. Durand was a member of a black-ops team, code- named "Shining Brass." The series depicts the horrific atrocities witnessed and performed by the once naïve special forces member as he attempts to perform his duties and understand the true meaning behind the madness. Durand's group was under the command of a combined force, comprised of every branch of the services, and headed up by the ever-popular Central Intelligence Committee. It's a journey into a shadow world of treachery and deceit—and reveals the way lives of Americans were traded about carelessly during the war in Vietnam.

ISBN: 978-1544962191 $14.99US

ABOVE AND BEYOND

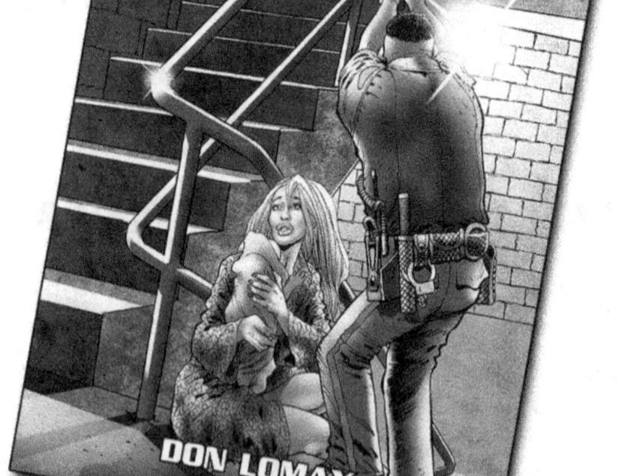
CALIBER COMICS PRESENTS
FROM THE FILES OF POLICE AND SECURITY NEWS:
ABOVE AND BEYOND
DON LOMAX

Beginning in May of 2007, noted comic writer and illustrator Don Lomax teamed up with Police and Security News magazine to produce the series "Above and Beyond" - real life depictions of heroic acts by law enforcement professionals. Just as our soldiers here and abroad deserve recognition for their unwavering service, so do the men and women who protect and serve the citizens of the United States. Contained within these pages are just a few stories of these individuals who have demonstrated selfless bravery and heroic action under the most difficult circumstances and gone above and beyond the call of duty.

ISBN: 978-1635299601 $ 9.99 US

WWW.CALIBERCOMICS.COM

ALSO AVAILABLE FROM CALIBER COMICS

QUALITY GRAPHIC NOVELS TO ENTERTAIN

THE SEARCHERS
VOLUME ONE
THE SHAPE OF THINGS TO COME

THE SEARCHERS: VOLUME 1

The Shape of Things to Come

Before *League of Extraordinary Gentlemen* there was *The Searchers*. At the dawn of the 20th Century the greatest literary adventurers from the minds of Wells, Doyle, Burroughs, and Haggard were created. All thought to be the work of pure fiction. However, a century later, the real-life descendents of those famous characters are recuited by the legendary Professor Challenger in order to save mankind's future. Series collected for the first time.

"Searchers is the comic book I have on the wall with a sign reading - 'Love books? Never read a comic? Try this one! ....money back guarantee...'" - Dark Star Books.

WAR OF THE WORLDS: INFESTATION

Based on the H.G. Wells classic! The "Martian Invasion" has begun again and now mankind must fight for its very humanity. It happened slowly at first but by the third year, it seemed that the war was almost over... the war was almost lost.

"Writer Randy Zimmerman has a fine grasp of drama, and spins the various strands of the story into a coherent whole... imaginative and very gritty."
- *war-of-the-worlds.co.uk*

THE WAR OF THE WORLDS
INFESTATION
ZIMMERMAN HORUS

HELSING
LEGACY BORN
GARY REED JOHN LOWE

HELSING: LEGACY BORN

From writer Gary Reed (Deadworld) and artists John Lowe (Captain America), Bruce McCorkindale (Godzilla). She was born into a legacy she wanted no part of and pushed into a battle recessed deep in the shadows of the night. Samantha Helsing is torn between two worlds...two allegiances...two families. The legacy of the Van Helsing family and their crusade against the "night creatures" comes to modern day with the most unlikely of all warriors.

"Congratulations on this masterpiece..."
- Paul Dale Roberts, Compuserve Reviews

DEADWORLD

Before there was The Walking Dead there was Deadworld. Here is an introduction of the long running classic horror series, Deadworld, to a new audience! Considered by many to be the godfather of the original zombie comic with over 100 issues and graphic novels in print and over 1,000,000 copies sold, Deadworld ripped into the undead with intelligent zombies on a mission and a group of poor teens riding in a school bus desperately try to stay one step ahead of the sadistic, Harley-riding King Zombie. Death, mayhem, and a touch of supernatural evil made Deadworld a classic and now here's your chance to get into the story!

DEADWORLD
REQUIEM FOR THE WORLD

DAYS OF WRATH

DAYS OF WRATH

Award winning comic writer & artist Wayne Vansant brings his gripping World War II saga of war in the Pacific to Guadalcanal and the Battle of Bloody Ridge. This is the powerful story of the long, vicious battle for Guadalcanal that occurred in 1942-43. When the U.S. Navy orders its outnumbered and out-gunned ships to run from the Japanese fleet, they abandon American troops on a bloody, battered island in the South Pacific.

"Heavy on authenticity, compellingly written and beautifully drawn."
- *Comics Buyers Guide*

THE BOBCAT

Described as the Native American *Black Panther*.
1898. Indian Territory. Will Firemaker is a Cherokee Blacksmith who is finding out that the world of ancient lore and myth of his Tribe, that Will had always thought of as tribal fairytales, are actually true, and they're telling him he must replace his best friend from the animal kingdom, The Great Cat, as the guardian of his people. This sends him down a path of shock and disbelief as beings from the ancient past begin to manifest themselves in the world of reality. And as malevolent forces rise up in the wake of the fledgling Industrial Age, the future rushes head on into the Old West. Tahlequah will never be the same...

THE BOBCAT
HOSTLER MEHSLING

ANTHOLOGY SERIES
CALIBER PRESENTS
VOLUME I

CALIBER PRESENTS

The original Caliber Presents anthology title was one of Caliber's inaugural releases and featured predominantly new creators, many of which went onto successful careers in the comics' industry. In this new version, Caliber Presents has expanded to graphic novel size and while still featuring new creators it also includes many established professional creators with new visions. Creators featured in this first issue include nominees and winners of some of the industry's major awards including the Eisner, Harvey, Xeric, Ghastly, Shel Dorf, Comic Monsters, and more.

LEGENDLORE

From Caliber Comics now comes the entire Realm and Legendlore saga as a set of volumes that collects the long running critically acclaimed series. In the vein of The Lord of The Rings and The Hobbit with elements of Game of Thrones and Dungeon and Dragons.

Four normal modern day teenagers are plunged into a world they thought only existed in novels and film. They are whisked away to a magical land where dragons roam the skies, orcs and hobgoblins terrorize travelers, where unicorns prance through the forest, and kingdoms wage war for dominance. It is a world where man is just one race, joining other races such as elves, trolls, dwarves, changelings, and the dreaded night creatures who steal the night.

LEGENDLORE
THE REALM CHRONICLES
TIME SLIP

TIME GRUNTS
VOLUME ONE: THE MONSTERS WITHIN

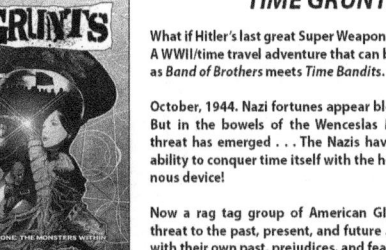

TIME GRUNTS

What if Hitler's last great Super Weapon was – Time itself! A WWII/time travel adventure that can best be described as *Band of Brothers* meets *Time Bandits*.

October, 1944. Nazi fortunes appear bleaker by the day. But in the bowels of the Wenceslas Mines, a terrible threat has emerged . . . The Nazis have discovered the ability to conquer time itself with the help of a new ominous device!

Now a rag tag group of American GIs must stop this threat to the past, present, and future . . . While dealing with their own past, prejudices, and fears in the process.

CALIBER COMICS

www.calibercomics.com

www.ingramcontent.com/pod-product-compliance
Lightning Source LLC
Chambersburg PA
CBHW081406070526
44583CB00020B/2706